THE REVOLUTIONARY ANTI-IMPERIALISM OF THE APOSTLE PAUL

Constructive Considerations for a Ghetto Theology

BLACK DIVINITY SERIES VOL 1

SHAHIDI ISLAM

Book Ordering Information
Cover design provided by: https://www.fiverr.com/patrick_2013
Email: shahidiislam@godbodyinternational.com
https://godbodyinternational.com

Attention African American Theologians!!!

What if Everything you Thought you Knew About the End Times Was Wrong?

Eschatological Judgments is the second instalment in Shahidi Islam's *Black Divinity Series*. With so many hyper-real and fantastical models for the end of the world is there another way to get to our truth. To learn more go to your online retailer now.

Eschatological Judgments

This book is dedicated to the Gods and
Goddesses of the foundation,
who dwell in a Nation of love, peace, and
happiness

Table of Contents

Series Preface

The current *Black Divinity Series* was originally written to create a new kind of Black theology: a Black Godbody Theology. The starting point for this theology is that all Black people are divine, yet this concept of Black divinity actually has a long history. It was first articulated by the ancient Ethiopians over twenty-eight millennia ago, in a land that was called in times past Ta Neteru (the land of the gods and goddesses). The message was then continued on in ancient Egypt by the various mystical traditions, around another nine millennia ago; and by the ancient Hebrew mystical traditions over three millennia ago. The message was eventually lost to the Hebrews during their many exiles, but it was still maintained in ancient Egypt and ancient Ethiopia over the vast centuries.

Then came the Baptist to revive among the Judeans the understanding of Black divinity. He would also start a liberation movement among the Judeans, predicting the coming of someone after him, in his own lifetime, who would bring the people back to their Black divinity through a baptism into holiness and into a fully independent monarchy. The very Messiah he prophesied, would continue on that message, which after his disappearance splintered off into several separate branches.

The mystics among his followers were called the gnostics and they combined the Messiah's message with the ancient Egyptian philosophy. The gnostic message thereby continued the idea of Black divinity secretly and underground during a time when even the mainstream messianic movement was also underground (due mainly to heavy persecution). Unfortunately, when the messianic movement, finally, did gain legality it was only the mainstream version. Gnosticism, however, would remain an outlaw movement, thus driving them even further underground.

At that time, within the mainstream movement the only Black person considered truly divine was the Messiah (back then the only images of the Messiah were as a Black man). Black divinity then re-emerged with Islamic mysticism, a tradition that combined the gnostic oral tradition with Islamic interpretations of the Quran. The Prophet himself was an ardent follower of gnostic ideas and beliefs. It is even likely that he was trained and mentored by a practicing gnostic. Whether this is true or not, we know for sure that he referenced several gnostic teachings and traditions in the Quran that he could not have possibly known without having some familiarity with their history.

Finally, Black divinity would ultimately reach its greatest height in America, starting with the Honorable Elijah Muhammad bringing to the Black communities of America that Islamic mystical tradition through his Lost-Found Nation of Islam. From the Nation of Islam would then eventually emerge the godbody movement: a movement in the ghetto that went on to define G.O.D. as guns over drugs—thereby interpreting that the militant Black man that gains Knowledge 120 becomes a God in his own right, having the power to give life (through spreading 120) and to take life (we all know how); and to build; and to destroy.

Now for the most part we try to use this power, not to take life, but to build through it a Nation of Gods and Earths (hereafter to be called Goddesses).

That said, the 120 lessons we godbodies endorse are, again, only just the Supreme Wisdom lessons of the Honorable Elijah Muhammad. In that sense they have been read and mastered by several heroes and heroines within the Black community including: Minister Louis Farrakhan, Minister Malcolm X, Imam Warith Deen Muhammad, Dr. Khalid Muhammad, Dr. Sebi Alfredo Bowman, Dr. Malachi Z. York, the Champ Muhammad Ali, Erikah Badu, Bilal the 1st Born, D'Angelo, Jay Electronica, Busta Rhymes, Rakim Allah, Nas, Foxy Brown, Queen Latifah, all of the Fugees, the Wu-Tang Clan, Mobb Deep, and Brand Nubian. Even so, while the United States government has attacked and attempted to discredit many of these Black leaders, all of them are still well beloved by most Black people. The truth is, we Black people have always had the potential for divinity, but it is only now that we are starting to realise how to actually achieve it.

True, it may be currently accepted among the godbody — again, the ghetto organisation that is currently the central body propagating the message of Black divinity — that once a city, a nation, and the world comes to accept the truth of our destiny then a Black thearchy will begin to exist upon the earth. Indeed, as any true solarpunk/ecofuturist would much rather aim and strive for a low-tech and high-empath future; even so, within the godbody a more ghetto combination of solarpunk and Neo-Soul is believed to be more desirable; but that mainly through Black people taking their place as a God-Collective of the divine Black people we have always been.

Series Introduction

The current series is based on notes originally written in 2006 and edited in 2012 and again in 2019 for the purpose of liberating my people. Contained within are also a very large cross-section of quotations that break up a lot of the content making it seem at times frustrating and a little hard to read. This annoyance was unavoidable due to the current situation, and the unfortunate mistrust of those outside of the street life of the intelligence of anyone arising out of the street life. Again, hopefully no one within the street life, particularly within the Five Percent Nation, will be too offended by some of the language that I have chosen to use throughout, as it was mainly for the purpose of speaking to the uninitiated, not to ruin our image or desecrate our culture.

From an historical context all past developments in human progress have been correlated to philosophical precursors. From Aristotle's influence on ancient Greece and Plato's influence over the Roman *res publica*; to the influence of Rousseau on the French Revolution and Marx on the Russian; it is virtually impossible to separate historical epochs from their philosophical precursors. The initial philosophical bursts of light and hope, however, usually begin to dim as the pains of reaction begin to set in. This reactionary response to the new ideas and the hostility of its opposition usually bring great sorrow and disillusionment to the representatives of the new vision and ideal.

As these realities are the historical norm for all prior to revolutionary changes it is clear that anything of this calibre will meet also its own huge bursts of reactionary opposition and rage. From church pulpit to political gathering, from social clubs to cultural events all groups and sections of society claim allegiance to morality and against the dark cloud of the street life. True indeed, as the streets are considered a curse on society, and themselves cursed of God, we, in the eyes of those outside of the streets, should have nothing to do with anything even resembling the theocentric, let alone the thearchic. In fact, our anti-establishment makes us seem to any who are not affiliated to be more nihilistic than ritualistic. This anti-establishment being a product of our rejection by the establishment and being outcasts to it, has caused us to question our place in a society that would create and tolerate such vicious injustices as occur in the neighbourhoods of this so-called Western society.

But the Black thearchy itself is really just a system based on the identification of a new Black theodicy, that is, a study of God's goodness and righteousness from a Black person's perspective. Having arisen from the backstreets of New York as the godbody, we have taken their general outlook and message, and added to them theological, psychological, ideological, sociological, ecological, and cosmological depth. Conversely, though, the Black thearchy is primarily based on the use of godbody codes and culture to achieve Black identity amid the difficult and adverse situations of racism, poverty, humiliation, demonisation, dyseducation, discrimination, marginalisation, criminalisation, and state-orchestrated incarceration.

As a people most of we Blacks have been separated from our history and a knowledge of our history; but as Nature expresses herself through a cyclical rhythm of spontaneous repetitions, I feel that a knowledge of recent Black history is worth acknowledging. Marcus Garvey inspired an entire generation with the thought of a Black God. A God, not White like their slave-masters (or like their job-managers in this current system of wage-slavery) but a God Black like them, who understood the trials and sufferings of the people and offered them the strength and power to redeem themselves from these sufferings.

This philosophy spread in Africa, America, and the Caribbean in many forms. Two most obvious forms were the Rastafarians, who claimed Negusa Negast Tafari was the Black God incarnate, and the Black theologians, who claimed the Messiah Jesus was the Black God incarnate. But you also had the Black Muslims, who claimed Master Fard Muhammad was the Black God incarnate. Then you had the Afrocentrics who claimed the ancestral gods of Africa (particularly those of ancient Egypt), which manifest themselves in Nature, were the Black gods incarnate. Even the Kemetic scholars (who are commonly and derisively called "Hoteps" by most Black people) would claim the Egyptian god Ra to be the Black God incarnated in all Black males; similar to the Five Percent, who claim Allah to be *the God* incarnated in all Black males who have mastered the 120 lessons and opened the third eye of astral vision.

All that said, the basis for the current *Black Divinity Series* is six categorical systems which are instituted within the godbody movement to allow for our further continuance: Black divinity, Black revolutionism, Black eroticism, Black astralism, Black demodernisation, and Black syndicalism. These all effectively spell up to the words: Black DREADS; and all also make up the godbody ideology that I endorse —

and are generally accepted within the godbody movement as a whole – though they have never been spelled-out or outlined in this sort of way before. What I thereby hope to accomplish with this undertaking is a complete renewal of our movement and the lessons of the movement as handed down to me by my mentor and enlightener so as to show where our movement can lead and why the actual teleology of godbodyism will be a positive and not a self-destructive one.

In itself the godbody theory articulated throughout has been designed to be a form of Black ideology that incorporates ideas, language, and expressions from chaos theory, deconstruction theory, decolonising theory, post-colonial theory, critical race theory, pro-Black anarchist theory, and pro-sex womanist theory into the outlook and world vision of the Five Percent Nation. And as stated earlier the Five Percent Nation as a movement teaches that the Black man is God. Beginning in the 1960s under the leadership of a direct disciple of Malcolm X, who at that time was named Clarence 13X, but who we call Allah out of respect for the vision he received of the potential divinity of all Black men, obviously including himself, we seek also to enlighten our people as to their potential.

The traditions of the godbody movement founded by Allah are, again, based on the 120 lessons, which in themselves are really just the Supreme Wisdom lessons of the Honorable Elijah Muhammad. In that sense they have been read and mastered by several heroes and heroines within the Black community: Minister Louis Farrakhan, Minister Malcolm X, Imam Warith Deen Muhammad, Dr. Khalid Muhammad, Dr. Sebi Alfredo Bowman, Dr. Malachi Z. York, Muhammad Ali, Jay Electronica, Busta Rhymes, Erikah Badu, Ice Cube, Rakim Allah, Nas, Mobb Deep, the Wu-Tang Clan, and Brand Nubian. Furthermore, while the

United States government has attacked and attempted to discredit many of these Black leaders here mentioned, all of them are still well beloved by the Black community in general.

Nevertheless, my central cause for rewriting *Black Divinity* as a series was not just so as to create a new ideology and sociology for Black people, but more so to make a kind of ghetto theology, a Black Godbody Theology, for our overall empowerment. It cannot be denied that the godbody has a theology as we all share a general theory of God, of the devil, and of righteousness. Yet, as an African American theology the godbody theology can still be differentiated from that of the classical model of African American theology. If we take as an example the four degrees of faith (Skousen 2017): from no faith, to little faith, to great faith, to complete faith, we can see that classical African American theology features most of these four levels: the humanists have no faith, the liberationists/womanists have great faith, and the prosperous have complete faith. Well, we godbodies complete the cipher by having little faith, believing God to exist mainly in natural phenomena like a Universal Intelligence, the Universal Laws, the Original Black man, and all Original people.

Basically, it is the aim and purpose of this book to represent the godbody movement by, firstly, seeking to introduce the godbody theology as an African American theology nuanced from Cone's in that it is not a survival theology but a thrival theology; a thrival theology that came out of the ghetto experience to give to the Black people of the ghetto the hope for a better future, one which they themselves create. Herein, Black Godbody Theology is a ghetto theology that promotes Black improvement and empowerment; even as James Cone himself stated, "Unless theology can become 'ghetto theology,' a theology that speaks to black people, the gospel message has no promise of life for the black man – it is a lifeless message" (Cone 2021: 37).

Even so, it must obviously also be noted that a lot of the ideas and practices encouraged throughout are not those of the entire godbody of the United States, but are add-ons I developed based on lessons I learned in the Socialist Workers Party as an anti-capitalist and in the Black Church as a Pentecostal. As I left America as a "newborn" godbody I never had the chance to fully master the 120 lessons; I did, however, take a lot of the lessons I learned in cipher with the godbody and expound on them to co-create with my enlightener: God Born Supreme Allah, a Black thearchy based on his own GBSA-ideology. This book therefore is mainly a union of all the previous movements I learned from so as to contribute to the further empowering of our people.

Recognising also that a lot of the Gods themselves have no tolerance for innovation; I concluded that we stand no hope of ever overthrowing White supremacy without making certain changes to our lessons. We will never elevate until we are willing to innovate. And if we were to find that something was emphatically wrong we would be obliged to destroy it and so elevate beyond it, even as we destroy the mathematics of anyone who does not backup their lessons with proof. It is my hope that these lessons, which are mainly based on quotations, can be used by all other newborns to understand how the Gods build, and by godbodies to bring us to a place of true divinity in our ways and actions based on knowledge, wisdom, and under-standing. True indeed, as the highest form of understanding is love, even so, the highest form of love is libidinal, it is by this kind of love that we will be able to elevate beyond local hood heroes to become global superheroes.

Finally, it is my intention for the current approach to be used to inform the course of the godbody movement in its rise to popularity, and to create an avenue for the acceptance of this theological perspective within the current discussions of African American theology. Within this context I pay homage to those who came before me in the classical schools: Anthony B. Pinn, William R. Jones, James H. Cone, Albert B. Cleage, Delores S. Williams, Kelly B. Douglas, Robert S. Beckford, Anthony G. Reddie, Creflo A. Dollar, and Thomas D. Jakes. Still, it must also be said at this point that although I am myself a fellow of the Society for the Study of Theology, all the ideas and outlooks presented in this book are overwhelmingly my own and nobody else's. Peace.

The Supreme Mathematics

Potentials

k = knowledge (1)

w = wisdom (2)

u = understanding (3)

f = freedom – I choose not to add culture as freedom is the most obvious elevation from understanding and culture is implied in the whole mathematics (4)

p = power – (I use the term power neither in the Marxian sense, as in to dominate nor in the Foucauldian sense, as in to discipline or surveille; but instead use it in the Adlerian sense as in empowerment) I choose not to add refinement as power is the next elevation from freedom and progresses till it reaches equality (5)

e = equality (6)

G = God – where God is equivalent to the omnipresent, and not to a state of pure perfection (7)

B = build – when adding on (8)

D = destroy – when subtracting (8)

$\forall$ = born (9)

° = cipher (0)

Symbols

D = dialectical moment where *pa* > *na* becomes *na* > *pa*, or vice versa.

Lm = the limitation

∃ = when there is

+ = together with

∈ = the sum includes

> = greater than

≥ = greater than or equal to

< = lesser then

≤ = lesser than or equal to

→ = leads on to

↔ = if and only if

↗ = on the increase

↘ = on the decrease

∝ = proportional to

Values

∞ = infinity

o = zero

λ = wavelength

A = amplitude

d = displacement

t = time expended

v = rate of velocity

δ = astral forces $->x^1$

α = social forces $->x^{10}$

β = global forces $->x^{20}$

θ = environmental forces $->x^{30}$

ϕ = terrestrial forces (also called geomagnetic forces) $->x^{40}$

ϑ = solar forces (also called heliospheric magnetic forces) $->x^{50}$

∂ = globular forces (also called stellar magnetic forces) $->x^{60}$

φ = galactic forces (also called galactic magnetic forces) $->x^{70}$

ψ = super-clusteral forces (also called intercluster magnetic forces) $->x^{80}$

$\mathcal{E} = $ cosmic forces $- > x^{90}$

$Pa = $ positive action of an individual

$pa = $ positive action of a social body

$Na = $ negative action of an individual

$na = $ negative action of a social body

$x = $ social potential of a social body

$n = $ level of social potentiality

$g = $ a social movement

$opp.\,g = $ an oppressing social movement

$emp.\,g = $ an empowering social movement

$(pa) = $ all the positive actions of a social body

$(na) = $ all the negative actions of a social body

$(v) = $ all the social velocity

$(g) = $ the whole social movement

$S = $ decelerative force caused by reaction of social body x_1

$R = $ accelerative force caused by resistance of social body x_2

$S = $ syndicalism

The Godbody System

The Universal Laws of Existence

1. The law of interaction (whose corollary is the pleasure principle),

2. The law of intersubjectivity (whose corollary is the vibratory law),

3. The law of self-organisation (whose corollary is the identity law),

4. The law of opposition (whose corollary is the polarity law),

5. The law of repetition (whose corollary is the inertia law),

6. The law of self-similarity (whose corollary is the correspondence law),

7. The law of conservation (whose corollary is the reciprocity law),

8. The law of evolution (whose corollary is the power law),

9. The law of devolution (whose corollary is the entropy law),

10. The law of self-destruction (whose corollary is the phase-transition law),

11. The law of interconnectivity (whose corollary is the synchronicity law), and

12. The law of interrelation (whose corollary is the eternalist law).

The 10 Principles

1. No God but Allah

2. No power imbalances

3. No non-authors

4. No non-fighters

5. No Divine fights alone

6. No problems handled in the Square should ever leave the Square

7. No marriage or marriages

8. No missing parliament meetings

9. No wearing underwear

10. No harassment or rape of any kind ever

What We Teach

1. That Black people are the Original people of the planet earth.

2. That Black people are the fathers and mothers of civilization.

3. That the science of Supreme Mathematics is the key to understanding man's relationship to the universe.

4. That Islam is a natural way of life, not a religion.

5. That education should be fashioned to enable us to be self sufficient as a people.

6. That each one should teach one according to their knowledge.

7. That the Black man is god and his proper name is ALLAH. Arm, Leg, Leg, Arm, Head.

8. That our children are our link to the future and they must be nurtured, respected, loved, protected and educated.

9. That the unified Black family is the vital building block of the nation.

The Hedgehog Concept (The Build Allah Square)

1. Eat, Train, Read, Write, and Share

The Core Concepts

1. Black divinity, Black revolutionism, Black eroticism, Black astralism, Black demodernisation, and Black syndicalism

The Physical Concepts

1. biophysics, quantum physics, molecular physics, geophysics, astrophysics, and digital physics

The Discursive Concepts

1. body, embody, and disembody

2. structure, infrastructure, and superstructure

3. subtle, subaltern, and subterranean

4. text, pretext, subtext, and context

5. discourse, discursive, pre-discursive, narrative, and performative

6. reality, surreality, sub-reality, hyper-reality, virtual-reality, and unreality

7. erase, absent, present, represent, reproduce, re-enact, legitimate, and counter

8. position, supposition, disposition, composition, superposition, opposition, exposition, and imposition

9. silence, distort, fabricate, exaggerate, implicate, explicate, delineate, propagate, and voice

The Chronological Concepts

1. historicism and historicity

2. linear-chronological and event-sequential

3. historical, ahistorical, prehistorical, and transhistorical

The Pneumatological Concepts

1. demonise and transfigure

2. divine, vampyre, and devil

3. elemental, environmental, and universal

4. foresight, insight, and hindsight

5. *Sebi*, *Nebi*, and *Obi*

6. astral, astral body, astral force, and astral plane

7. *Hakim*, *Karim*, *Rahim*, and Allah

8. Horu construct, Hethor construct, Ausar conscious, and Auset conscious

9. existent, pre-existent, co-existent, de-existent, and re-existent

10. resurrected, incorporated, *phantomised*, internalised, and exorcised

11. empathic, psychopathic, sociopathic, *monopathic, duopathic, polypathic,* and *panopathic*

12. empath, dark empath, supernova empath, true empath, quiet empath, psychic empath, super empath, sigma empath, and Heyoka empath

The Psychological Concepts

1. conscious and unconscious

2. libido and superego

3. inhibition, prohibition, and exhibitionism

4. object, selfobject, and objectify

5. subject, subjective, and intersubjective

6. trauma, complex, and therapy

7. power, empower, internalise, incorporate, and concretise

8. spectre, drive, constraint, ideal, and somatic

The Ideological Concepts

1. seduction, perverse seduction, and seductionism

2. sexualise, racialise, and criminalise

3. White superiority, White supremacy, and White privilege

4. acculturate, assimilate, integrate, and institutionalise

5. gaze, oppress, problematise, and deviate

6. shackling, unshackling, deshackling, and reshackling

7. typical, atypical, prototypical, and archetypal

8. institution, destitution, restitution, constitution, deconstitution, and reconstitution

9. sexual, asexual, heterosexual, homosexual, transsexual, intersexual, and hypersexual

10. modern, premodern, postmodern, late modern (liquid modern), anti-modern, and demodernise

11. colony, market-colony, industrial-colony, military-colony, penal-colony, settler-colony, spatial-colony, cultural-colony, corporeal-colony, mental-colony, epistemic-colony, counter-colony, neo-colony, and the Great United States Empire (GUSE)

The Sociological Concepts

1. embodied displacement (exile, migration, trans-migration, or tourism) and disembodied displacement (phantasy, fantasy, wish, dream, vision, imagination, or astral journey)

2. aetiology, teleology, and eschatology

3. locality, globality, and communality

4. ordination, subordination, and superordination

5. gnosis, prognosis, diagnosis, and epignosis

6. inertia, action, interaction (force), and act-species

7. interior, exterior, anterior, posterior, and ulterior

8. mechanic, elastic, static, kinetic, and dynamic

9. politics, geopolitics, biopolitics, necropolitics, transpolitics, hyper-politics, body-politics, racial-politics, and sexual-politics

The Sociological Axioms

1. The Axioms of Social Mechanics

a) $x > 1$

b) $v < 670,616,629$ mph

c) $v = \dfrac{d}{t}$

2. The Axioms of Social Force

a) $v\left(\dfrac{x^n}{x^n}\right) = \alpha$

b) $x_1 + R = Lm$ and $x_2 + S = Lm$

c) $\alpha > x^{10}$

3. The Axioms of Social Movements

a) $x_1 > x_2 \leftrightarrow x_2\alpha \searrow o$

b) $g \propto \alpha$

c) $g_1(pa) \rightarrow g_2(na)$ and $g_1(na) \rightarrow g_2(pa)$

d) $d = (2\pi) \times \left(\frac{2\lambda + 2A}{2}\right)$

4. The Axioms of Social Kinetics

a) $x_1 + x_2 \to na$

b) $x_1 + x_2 \to pa \leftrightarrow Lm \searrow$

c) $pa > Lm \to D \leftrightarrow pa \searrow$

5. The Axioms of Social Statics

a) $g(Lm) \leftrightarrow \alpha \searrow o$

b) $\exists \alpha \searrow o \to x^u \geq g$

6. The Axioms of Social Dynamics

a) $Lm > g$

b) $\exists(\alpha > Lm) \to g \nearrow$

c) $\exists Lm \to \alpha \searrow + g \searrow$

Preface of Book

The book you are about to read focuses primarily on presenting to the reader the depths of certain godbody structures and ideas, using *observant participation* (Wacquant 2008) as its primary source. In particular it centres on godbody lessons that I learned during my experiences in both Brooklyn, New York and London, England, and the guidance I was given from my mentor and enlightener within the godbody movement. A man who himself is currently doing time in prison for a crime he did not commit.

The book was also written as part of a much broader book, carrying with it the central purpose of representing the New York City street culture and revealing some of its remarkable ideas to the Black intelligentsia of America. However, as I found it ever more difficult to get a footing in this crowd and among this audience I decided to rethink my original plan. Finding instead a home among African professionals I considered it far more necessary to remove some of the more immature and gang related themes of the original content and repackage it as a theology. My main objective at this time, at least with the current endeavour, is now to expound in detail the various aspects of this unique ghetto movement. A movement that has created a cultural mechanism so effective that it has changed the face and shape of the ghetto youth of the American East Coast and Black American underclass to this very day.

I do not want the reader to be confused though, the book as a whole must be read from a Christian perspective. The Islamic and Five Percent leanings do not in any ways compensate for the heavy Christian undertones expounded throughout. Nevertheless, the heart and soul of the book is to lead to a new interpretation of life and the Hebrew prophecies thereby bringing us to a place of fulfilment and salvation. Not that some outside saviour comes from the sky and saves us. Our salvation is self-performed. We become our own saviours through knowledge of self, love of self, and love of neighbour as of self. In this is found the kingdom God promised to the Hebrew people, and is also found the pathway to that divine nature that is opened up to us by accepting the message of truth.

These are all lessons articulated within the godbody movement. However, if we as a movement truly wish to be accepted within the mainstream we will be therefore in duty bound to explain to the bourgeois and intellectuals among our Black brothers and sisters just what it is that we are really all about in a detailed theological treatise so as to gain their support in maintaining our own doctrinal and cultural identity. It must therefore be acknowledged, as we proceed further into this discourse, that the thearchic movement being presented and re-presented throughout is a form of anarcho-Islamism. It is, however, only Islamist in the sense of being based on a revolutionary Islam, not in the sense of being terroristic – as most godbodies themselves are anti-terrorism and supra-religious.

This book was, finally, also written for my Sun and enlightener: God Born Supreme Allah, as a thank you for the jewels he dropped on me: these are what brought me to the light of truth. And to all the Gods and Earths out there, peace – coming straight from the God Shahidi Islam.

General Introduction

Following I will be exploring what I consider to be just concerning the name of Paul, even as the misuse and twisting of his teachings and very revolutionary ideas by that which is called the Pauline school has led to his current notoriety in the world as of capitalistic sensitivities. Choosing instead to consider what in Paul's life and work contains the kernel of his reality and avoiding all mystifying and otherworldly debates, I will be, in essence, trying to recapture that social theory that Paul implanted, or tried to implant, into his early followers and associates. It is my hope that in doing this I may return us to the core reality of the apostle Paul's very revolutionary vision for social change. Indeed, whether intentionally or unintentionally, the apostle Paul brought into the heart of mainstream society a kind of subaltern ethics whereby the colonised subjects of his time could identify themselves. It is through this prism of subalternality that we can trace the silences, the hidden truths and ideas that go unsaid, whether due to common comprehension or governmental regulation, that unlock the true ideals that the apostle Paul envisaged.

Many Christians today, especially among Evangelicals and Charismatics, use the apostle Paul as an excuse to justify their greed. Of all the apostles he has been considered the most liberal, and certainly he needed business affairs to run smoothly as he was also a tentmaker (Acts 18: 1-3). But was the apostle Paul's vision really for a capitalist world system as so many prosperity preachers claim it was, or is there in fact, hidden in the depths, the subterranean dungeons of this incessant political prisoner, an anarchic and anti-colonialist vision for social change. True, colonialism in the modern sense did not exist in the days of the apostle Paul, nevertheless, I shall be using the term throughout this series so as to allow the reader to understand and familiarise themselves with the reality of Paul's hope to produce within the readers of his letters a mental and bodily decolonisation from the then form of Western imperialism.

In its current form the world cannot afford to maintain the Western empire of implacable wealth creation. Competition inevitably turns into conflict, now open, now hidden conflict. It cannot but cause ruin because it is so disorderly and filled with contradictions. As István Mészáros pointed out, one of the contradictions which will prove to be, and has proven to be in the past, one of capital's absolute limits (capital being the means of production and exchange); is the contradiction between capital's national protectionism and its need to create transnational markets. Capital is of necessity private, personal, and nationalistic yet it needs to become international to maintain a prosperous existence. The imperialistic tendencies within capital cause its national manifestation to seek the overpowering of other national capitals; yet it must itself maintain this international dominance to keep from competitive obsolescence.

This contradiction existed during the times of early modern colonialism. In those times, capital's nationalist tendencies triumphed over its internationalist tendencies to a certain extent; which caused the liberation movements to fight for national sovereignty instead of international anarchy. But this internationalist tendency within capitalism has not gone away; instead it has re-emerged as globalised capital; a globalisation that has provided fuel for the fire of its critics hostility.

Modern Western imperialism in the twenty-first century currently has had only two substantial opponents: (i) the anti-imperialists and (ii) the Islamists. The anti-imperialists are usually post-colonialists as they were at one time subject to the early modern West in the form of colonialism. For the most part they now fear a neo-colonial advance from the West as they hear them preaching globalisation, but practicing the subjugation of smaller countries under the national capital, rules, and power structure of more modernised countries. Based on the practice of the West, and not their preaching, these countries, having nationalised their governments, would go on to nationalise a number of big properties for the native population of their location.

These countries, again, mostly post-colonialist, usually believe that all national capital should be held within the nation and shared out among the people of that nation. They are unfortunately too small or weak to fight a substantial war with the neoliberal neo-colonial powers, so as potential profit margins and the possibility of gaining some desired resource could always cause the West to fight if diplomacy ceases to work, threats of overthrow or assassination are usually more than enough to keep them in line or from going too far against the wishes of their Western overlords.

With Islamism it is a different story. First of all, Islamism is not, and should not be considered, a pejorative term for terrorism – most Islamists are anti-terrorist, it is only the Jihadists that usually resort to terrorism, but I will discuss more on this subject in a later book – most Muslims simply define Islamism as: revolutionary Islam. So, considering now, therefore, the expansion of Western legal and political dominance around the world, and the globalisation of consumerism and commodification into Islamic countries. Plus the extreme lack of morality in the articulated doctrines of modernism, especially by the standards held within those Muslim countries. These have all coalesced to cause the religious communities of those Muslim countries to rise up in rebellion. So far this has led to religious wars between America, the bearers of modernism, and certain of those Muslim nations, as the keepers of religious purity. They war with America mainly due to Western oppressive tendencies and extreme lack of moral purity, whereas America fights back in the name of anti-terrorism.

This may explode into world war in the current clash of ideologies – especially considering the genocidal and imperialistic tendencies of Zionism towards its surrounding Muslim neighbours – and even though America (a key supporters of Zionism) may be the current global superpower, in a battle with a morally superior opponent they cannot win. The immorality of their neo-colonisation and White supremacy, which they maintain with the force of both weaponry and technology, will one day have to give way to a new morality. The so-called "gods" of the current system are lost in an ideological struggle with each other. Western modernisation must snatch up as much of the world in an imperialistic scrabble for territory as it can before these territories begin their own fight back in the form of global war. It is from here that we are able to see the apostle Paul as representing the intersection of both anti-modern views.

The Ghetto Saviour and the Game of Life

In order to understand the truth about the apostle Paul in his historical context, there is a fundamental issue that is extremely important for us to recognise first: this issue is that the Judeans of the apostle Paul's day were not like the Jews we have today. Virtually all Muslims and some enlightened Black people know that the original Judeans were themselves Black. That is, kind of dusky bronze (Black) in colour, as was said by the prophet Ezekiel, "In visions of God brought he me into the land of Israel, and set me upon a very high mountain, by which was as the frame of a city on the south. And he brought me thither, and, behold, there was a man, whose appearance was like the appearance of brass, with a line of flax in his hand, and a measuring reed; and he stood in the gate" (Ezekiel 40: 2, 3). Now the word translated here as brass is *nekhosheth*, which actually means copper, thus being in similitude to mahogany, and nowhere near the olive colour most Israelis have today. The implication from this Scripture is that the man is either a man of Israel or an angel of the God of Israel, either way he would have been the most likely colour of the historical people of Israel.

Yet if that is the case then why are the current Jews White? If we honestly wish to learn the truth we must begin by tracing the steps of Jose Malcioln, who himself found, "In 1941 Abraham

N. Poliak, an eminent Jewish scholar, born in Kiev in 1910, arrived in Palestine with his family determined to make a valuable contribution to Eretz Israel. Poliak was appointed professor of Medieval Jewish History at Tel Aviv University. He had read the true history of the origins and amalgamations of the original Hebrews and other tribes who lived in that area after the Flood. Qualified, secure, honest, and dignified as a scholar pursuing evidence to publish truth, Poliak read the books in Sabean, Cushitic, Aramaic, Arabic, and Hebrew. He then began publishing his findings in many books. In 1941, Professor Poliak wrote a book titled *The Khazar Conversion to Judaism!* His work appeared in a Hebrew publication called Zion."

So now, who were these Khazars he spoke of and why are they even important? According to Malcioln, "The Khazars … were of Turkish-Caucasoid origin. Germany, Poland and Russia are replete with the descendants of these people whose forefathers converted to Judaism for political expediency rather than because of religious fervor. The Khazars did not speak Hebrew during the time of their conversion. They visited the Turks requesting to be taught Hebrew. The Turks advised them to visit the Greeks because they did not know the language either. … The Greeks, who had been visiting and studying in Africa, and transporting information to Greece, taught the Khazars Hebrew and Torah" (Malcioln 1996: 90).

In continuing the narrative, eminent anthropologist Roland Dixon had this to say, "The Khazar being converted to Judaism in the eighth century, thereafter seem to have spread far and wide to the west and northwest, their modern descendants probably forming the preponderant element among the east European Jews." Malcioln further contributed that at their origins, "The Khazars [themselves] were interconnected through a confederation of tribes controlled by the Khagan or leader." Yet as of the eighth century he realised that his people would need to accept a monotheistic tradition, "The Khagan and his ruling class were clear on the issue. He and the top echelon knew the military power of the Caliph of Baghdad. If they chose Islam, they would be subjugated by the Caliphate according to the Islamic laws. If the Khazars chose Christianity, they would be equally subjugated by the Roman Emperor and dominated by his laws through the cross. So the majority of Khazar pagans followed their leader and the nobility, who selected Judaism to avoid subordination."

At this point, it could now be asked: What does all this have to do with anything? Well, according to Malcioln the "products of the Khazaric, Slavic, Turkish, Teutonic admixtures with even Magyars, commonly called Ashkenazim or European Jews," "went on to Western Germany, with some groups continuing on to Austria, through, and to, Bohemia, Hungary, Poland, Lithuania, Belorussia, and the Ukraine." But as we have already noted, these Ashkenazim were not authentic Jews and thereby never had the right to call themselves Semitic, even as we find written in the biblical Scriptures: "Now these are the generations of the sons of Noah, Shem, Ham, and Japheth: and unto them were sons born after the flood. The sons of Japheth; Gomer, and Magog, and Madai, and Javan, and Tubal, and Meshech, and Tiras. And the sons of Gomer; Ashkenaz, and Riphath, and Togarmah" (Genesis 10:1-3). Ashkenaz was always Japhethic.

Moreover, Malcioln further explicated the theory of Salmon Reinach that, "'The Hebrews [actually] made their first appearance in History as nomads.' Abraham, their patriarch, is said to have crossed the Jordan every Friday night – the Sabbath eve – to preach monotheism to the people of Canaan." Furthermore, this was all at a time "when Babylonia, Ethiopia, and Arabia were ruled by Africans." (Now obviously, the Arabs themselves, as descendants of Abraham, could not possibly have dominated Arabia, Egypt, or Babylonia in those days like they currently do today so the most likely inhabitants of all those lands was actually Black Africans). He further continued that it was around about that time that those who were "converted (including Abraham himself), went to Egypt, in Africa, abandoning Palestine and looking farther south. When they reached Ethiopia, the Egyptians and other Africans called them 'Falashim,' meaning strangers or foreigners."

Malcioln further went on to articulate how, "Several men [from among them that were] able to read and translate the Egyptian hieroglyphics and Ethiopic alphabet began writing contemporary history. Some copied the predictions of the sages from the walls of tombs, shrines, obelisks, and pyramids. Others wrote prophecies and laws. These writers were called prophets. Their collection of short and long stories copied from Egyptians and Babylonians was called the Bible … Before that, a part of it was called *Torah.* Their compilation of history, myths, predictions, laws, and admonitions became chapters or 'books.' … Thus, the Falashas [effectively] became known as 'the People of the Book.'" Here, ultimately revealing effectively that the original and authentic Hebrews of Canaan, Egypt, Arabia, Ethiopia, and Babylonia during its ancient history, and even deep into its early Islamic history, were most decisively a Black people.

Based on further deep research into the subject, Malcioln explained how, after the Falashas returned to the land of Canaan with Moses, a lot of them chose to remain behind in Egypt and Ethiopia. They became known throughout East Africa as the Agaw (the original Ge'ez Falashim that can be traced back to Abraham). Some tribes, however, began to migrate again out of Canaan land to further destinations. As noted, some "black-skinned members of the priesthood ran back to Egypt where they had gained the knowledge of religion and the key to the mystery system. Others ran to Tehemu, or Libya, where masonry was practiced, and eastern Cyrenaica, Mumidia, or Algiers, and Tunisia." Most of these became either Tuareg or Sephardic tribes; some travelling as far as Turkey, Sicily, France,

Spain, and Portugal, and after various, in some cases, forced intermarriages with the Europeans, formed the more lighter-skinned Sephardi in the world today.

Some of them, however, migrated to East Africa from Canaan forming the Kyla (said to have descended from the tribe of Ephraim) and the Amhara (said to have descended from the lineage of Solomon). Some of them went down south to Arabia and Yemen, and from there went even further south to southern Africa and Mozambique. Most of these became either Zagwe (said to have descended from Moses and his Ethiopian – most likely Oromo – wife) or the Lemba (said to have descended from the Levitical priesthood) tribes. Finally, some migrated as far west as Senegal and Mauritania founding and governing several great empires in West Africa including, but not limited to, the Ghana Empire, the Mali Empire, and the Songhai Empire. Within the last of these were included: the Fulani ethnicity, the Ashanti kingdom, the Judan kingdom, the Wenchi kingdom, the Dahomey kingdom, the Yoruba kingdom, and the Igbo kingdom.

Nevertheless, Malcioln also took note that, "In 1870 a French Jew named Joseph Halevy visited the Falashas. He was studying the languages of the various African tribes when he met this unusual group observing Hebrew customs and religious practices. The Falashas informed Halevy that they were the only Hebrews left in the world. They had not come in contact with any other Hebrews or Jews for centuries. The Falashim's Torah was [also] written in Ge'ez. This sociolinguistic find was announced by Halevy as the 'discovery of the Falashas.'" However, something far more diabolical was at play. Due to the high volume of intermarriages among the European Jews, both Ashkenazi and Sephardi, many Jews of the nineteenth century understood the precarious position their Judaism was in. For this cause, in order to authenticate themselves as Jews they had no further recourse but to return to their traditions. As most

Jews were well informed, sometime after the Neo-Babylonian Empire many of the ancient Falashic Hebrews were scattered to the four winds of heaven, though some of them were chosen by the Persian Emperor Cyrus to rebuild their fallen temple and re-establish their lost traditions.

That said, according to Islamic tradition, by the time those Hebrews returned to do so the Amorites had already destroyed most of the authentic copies of the Tawrat. It was therefore up to those scholars and lawyers, who had committed the Tawrat to memory to accomplish the task. However, unbeknownst to them at the time, copies of the true and authentic Tawrat had been kept preserved in Ethiopia and Saba for centuries. Herein we find that Halevy's intentions may not have been so noble as to simply find, or even preserve, African traditional cultures. Moreover, according to the Jewish Encyclopedia of 1959, Halevy "taught at schools of the Alliance Israelite Universelle in Turkey and Rumania and in 1868, went at the request of the Alliance to Ethiopia where he visited the Falashas. Subsequently, the Academic des Inscriptions et Belles Lettres sent him to Yemen where, disguised as a native rabbi, he succeeded in collecting 686 Sabean inscriptions (1869-70)."

What this shows is, basically, at the request of those "credible academic bodies" Halevy, through deception and dishonesty, was instructed to smuggle and steal various Sabean documents and thereby to learn and teach various true and authentic Hebrew customs and traditions. Indeed, these Sabean documents were obviously urgently needed by the European Jews in order to learn the authentic liturgy, customs, and rituals of the Sabean Hebrews. But this also, at the same time, undermines the authenticity of their own Hebraism. For if they truly considered their own Hebraism to have been authentic there would have been no need for all the subterfuge. Thereby proving that the true and authentic Hebrews were actually the Falashism.

None of this means we Black people should hate the Ashkenazim for appropriating one of our religions. It does, however, mean the Ashkenazim must acknowledge what their ancestors did and stop denying it as merely anti-Semitic propaganda. It also means the apostle Paul's journey to self-discovery must have been a very interesting and even complex one, with all the racial minefields he must have traversed. We can even get glimpses of its depths scattered throughout his letters in the biblical tradition. From this biblical account the little information we gather about his life before joining the messianic movement are such: Paul was born Saul in the city of Tarsus in modern-day Turkey. He was a Benjamite Judean, and still most likely a Black man, however, he was also tellingly born a citizen of the city of Rome.

From this little information we can gather that Paul was bought up in a middle class family from two places; the fact that he was born a citizen of Rome even though he was Judean by race and the fact that Tarsus was famed by early authors such as Strabo for being a very wealthy place filled with intellectuals as well as aristocrats. Saul then obviously went on to learn Judaism as well as philosophy as an apprentice, a truth we can gather from his letters' almost Platonian style. Saul was bought up a Pharisee. And although he was born in Tarsus, the accounts in Acts say he was bought up in Jerusalem and was mentored in the way of the Torah by Rabbi Gamaliel. So Saul apparently had a good Judaic upbringing from Tarsus to Jerusalem. And from Paul's own testimony we find that he also persecuted the messianic communities when they first began popping up.

This same Saul, as most Christians would know, was converted because while he was on his way to Damascus to persecute the messianic communities there, he received a vision of the risen Messiah and was blinded. Then, it was a follower of the messianic tradition who opened his eyes to see again, converting and baptising him into the messianic movement.

Saul, from that moment, went through a real humbling. It is very reminiscent of the conversion of Malcolm X, a pimp, a hustler, and a thief, who went on to found several Muslim temples in America for the Nation of Islam.

Malcolm X's conversion story is a little less well known than that of the apostle Paul's. Malcolm Little was arrested in Boston for theft and was given a ten year sentence. During the majority of his time, of which he served seven years before being paroled to his brother, his family was able to convince him they could get him out of prison. At this time Malcolm had become so depraved that the other inmates called him Satan. He would argue with the correction officers and chaplains and would pretend he forgot his prison number to get put into solitary. Malcolm's Damascus experience is when his brother told him he knew a man, a Black man, who had $360°$ of knowledge. Soon, in a vision Malcolm would see this man as Master Fard Muhammad, the founder of the Nation of Islam. Like with Saul Malcolm was humbled and devoted the rest of his time in prison to studying and learning about the Nation of Islam. By the time he was released he was still not ready yet to preach, but, just like Saul, when the time was right Malcolm could not be stopped.

Malcolm Little was given the name Malcolm X by the Nation of Islam just as Saul was given the name Paul by the messianic movement. This messianic movement, predominantly being filled with Black Judeans, predominantly being filled with peasant farmers and non-industrialised workers, shared many similarities with the early Nation of Islam. Messianism as a movement started out among the lower classes, then grew to gain aristocrats and merchants, and soon people from all walks of life. Thus, Paul became a poor righteous teacher in the early messianic movement even as Malcolm X would become in the Islamic national movement. But none of Paul's teachings say the kind of social system he believed God would approve of. To him the kingdom of God (or Nation of God) was imminent –

even Malcolm X shared a similar feeling of imminence about the Nation of Islam – but unlike most of his messianic contemporaries, his form of anti-imperialism was not through violent sedition but through ethical progression.

At the height of his influence he wrote to the messianic communities of Rome, saying, "I am not ashamed of the gospel of Christ: for it is the power of God unto salvation to everyone that believeth; to the Jew first, and also to the Greek" (Romans 1: 16). As, in the apostle Paul's time, these Jews he spoke of were still predominantly Black, when Paul said things like, "to the Jew first, and also to the Greek", he was actually saying to the Black first and also to the White, he was naming the full spectrum of racial orientation. The apostle Paul was a Black man and as a Black man he understood the realities of the Black struggle. The sufferings he experienced as a Judean in imperial Rome were the sufferings of a Black man in a White world system.

Malcolm X's understanding of the racial dichotomy was relatively different. Though Malcolm X accepted that in the struggle of the races, the Black was first, in his consideration of the White man he felt more sure of their overthrow and judgment. Malcolm X wrote, "The Honorable Elijah Muhammad teaches us that since Western society is deteriorating, it has become overrun with immorality, and God is going to judge it, and destroy it. And the only way the black people caught up in this society can be saved is not to *integrate* into this corrupt society, but to *separate* from it, to a land of our own, where we can reform ourselves, lift up our moral standards, and try to be godly." Thus, the kingdom of God, for him, as a separatist, was in a separated land where Black people could practice Islam freely, with justice and ethics.

The apostle Paul's own insistence on justice and ethics was also based on his understanding that with an imminent kingdom of God, judgment was going to rain down on the enemies of God. In perilous determination he pointed out that not only salvation but also tribulation began with the Jews and continued on to the Greeks. "For the Jews require a sign, and the Greeks seek after wisdom: But we preach Christ crucified, unto the Jews a stumblingblock, and unto the Greeks foolishness; But unto them which are called, both Jews and Greeks, Christ the power of God, and the wisdom of God." Again, where it said wisdom the word used was *sophia*, as in philo*sophia* and the word he used for power was *dynamis*, as in dynamism. The judgment given to each would be based on their own interpretation of the actuality of God, particularly in his manifestation as the crucified Messiah. Still, this tells us nothing of the desired social programme God, from the apostle Paul's perspective, sought for.

Justice and ethics can obviously be discerned in his doctrine. However, that is not to say there was no contradiction, though we also read in the apostle Paul, "The just shall live by faith. And the law is not of faith: but, The man that doeth them shall live in them", justice by faith also proves to be a vain standard to fear without knowing that in which you are placing your faith. For if you place your faith in vanity to walk after that, the corruption of "sin is at the door" and it will master you. And if you put your faith in the flesh (that is, the material world) to walk after that, "the end thereof is death" and there is no coming back from that.

Malcolm X's own predilection toward justice and ethics was due to him realising, "The black man in the ghettoes … has to start self-correcting his own material, moral and spiritual defects and evils. The black man needs to start his own program to get rid of drunkenness, drug addiction, prostitution. The black man in America has to lift up his own sense of values." He also recognised that it would be the extent of our self-awareness that would allow us to come to the full conclusion of our place in society: "My black brothers and sisters – *no* one will know *who* we are … until *we* know who we are! We never will be able to *go* anywhere until we know *where* we are! The Honorable Elijah Muhammad is giving us a true identity, and a true position – the first time they have ever been *known* to the American black man!" Thus the consideration of the Black predicament is, and was to people like the apostle Paul and Malcolm X, based on the self-awareness of Black people as to their condition.

When Her Poker Face Destroys His Flush

"For as many of you as have been baptized into Christ have put on Christ. There is neither Jew nor Greek, there is neither bond nor free, there is neither male nor female: for ye are all one in Christ Jesus." This exclamation of the apostle Paul's, at one time undermined, but also distorted, the social fields of contest and socio-political embodiment that existed for decades in imperial Rome. On the other hand, it was also a contextual mantra that eliminated all the ideological oppositions of the world: the ever faithful Manichaean conflicts. The first social field of contest that we shall explore following will be the gender conflict. Here the apostle Paul is not believed by most people, misogynist or feminist alike, to have really contributed anything towards the empowerment of women; but in fact to have actively encouraged their subjugation and subordination within both the messianic movement and within society at large.

However, the truths of positions and opinions can also, more definitively be discovered in the silences of history; those records and presentations not memorialised or contested. It is in these kinds of records that we can find the apostle Paul's true opinions about women in the messianic movement. For example, the apostle Paul wrote to the messianic community at Corinth, "Nevertheless neither is the man without the woman, neither the woman without the man, in the Lord. For as the woman is of the man [in regard to the need for spermatisation], even so is the man also by the woman [in regard to the need for gestation and deliverance]; but all things of God" (1Corinthians 11: 11, 12). Such is a different picture entirely to the one painted historically by the definitively misogynistic Western leaders, or even the feminists who have accepted their interpretations as fact and simply sought to invert or subvert them.

True, even this sexual egalitarianism can be problematised, especially in that it is said concerning the apostle Paul, that he essentially sought to control women's body politics and sexual politics, as the apostle Paul wrote to the messianic communities of Rome, "For this cause God gave them up unto vile affections: for even their women did change the natural use into that which is against nature" (Romans 1: 26). These ideas, especially in the imperial metropolis, had an air of the moralistic, and even the legalistic, about them. Obviously, the apostle Paul's homo-phobia is legendary, yet perhaps it is also overstated. The translators of the Bible played a much larger role in this apparent truth than anything else. For example, the word translated here as natural was the Greek word *physikos* which could also translate as instinctual, and "against nature" (*paraphysis*) can translate to sterile or to something more contextual like: inhibit the instincts.

Paul is, nevertheless, continually critiqued on his thirst to control women's body politics and bodily performances, particularly with regard to their mode of dress, which is viewed as to highlight and demarcate their subordinate position. Indeed, the apostle Paul did write, "Every man praying or prophesying, having his head covered, dishonoureth his head. But every woman that prayeth or prophesieth with her head uncovered dishonoureth her head: for that is even all one as if she were shaven. For if the woman be not covered, let her also be shorn: but if it be a shame for a woman to be shorn or shaven, let her be covered".

Conversely, what was being implied in the subtext of this verse was the apostle Paul's acknowledgment that women *could actually* lead prayer and *could actually* prophesy. Moreover, these kinds of regulatory practices and ideas were not unique to the apostle Paul or to first century behaviour. Even the Prophet said in the Quran, "Say to the believing men that they lower their gaze and restrain their sexual passions. That is purer for them. Surely Allah is Aware of what they do. And say to the believing women that they lower their gaze and restrain their sexual passions and do not display their adornment except what appears thereof. And let them wear their head-coverings over their bosoms. And they should not display their adornment except to their husbands or their fathers, or the fathers of their husbands, or their sons, or the sons of their husbands, or their brothers, or their brothers' sons, or their sisters' sons, or their women, or those who their right hands possess, or guileless male servants, or the children who know not women's nakedness. And let them not strike their feet so that the adornment that they hide may be known. And turn to Allah all, O believers, so that you may be successful" (Quran 24: 30, 31).

Furthermore, contrast these readings with the fabled, "Moreover the Lord saith, Because the daughters of Zion are haughty, and walk with stretched forth necks and wanton eyes, walking and mincing as they go, and making a tinkling with their feet: Therefore the Lord will smite with a scab the crown of the head of the daughters of Zion, and the Lord will discover their secret parts." But "Fear not; for thou shalt not be ashamed: neither be thou confounded; for thou shalt not be put to shame: for thou shalt forget the shame of thy youth, and shalt not remember the reproach of thy widowhood any more. For thy Maker is thine husband; the Lord of hosts is his name; and thy Redeemer the Holy One of Israel; The God of the whole earth shall he be called." So, "Let us be glad and rejoice, and give honour to him: for the marriage of the Lamb is come, and his wife hath made herself ready. And to her was granted that she should be arrayed in fine linen, clean and white: for the fine linen is the righteousness of saints" (Revelations 19: 7, 8).

Again, as the Messiah said also,

> *"The kingdom of heaven is like unto a certain king, which made a marriage for his son, And sent forth his servants to call them that were bidden to the wedding: and they would not come. Again, he sent forth other servants, saying Tell them which are bidden, Behold. I have prepared my dinner: my oxen and my fatlings are killed, and all things are ready: come unto the marriage. But they made light of it, and went their ways, one to his farm, another to his merchandise: and the remnant took his servants, and entreated them spitefully, and slew them. But when the king heard thereof, he was wroth: and he sent forth his armies, and destroyed those murderers, and burned up their city. Then saith he to his servants, The wedding is ready, but they which were bidden were not worthy. Go ye therefore into the highways, and as many as ye shall find, bid to the marriage. So those servants went out into the highways, and gathered together all as many as they found, both bad and good: and the wedding was furnished with guests. And when the king came in to see the guests, he saw there a man which had not on a wedding garment: And he saith unto him, Friend, how camest thou in hither not having a wedding garment? And he was speechless. Then said the king to the servants, Bind him hand and foot, and take him away, and cast him into outer darkness: there shall be weeping and gnashing of teeth" (Matthew 22: 2-13).*

There is clearly hidden meaning in these cultural articulations and dress-codes, meanings lost in the colonial appropriation of the dominant culture. Yet these codes, meanings, and their embodiments can be rediscovered through an identification of the hidden silences of history. Thus in the apostle John's saying, "And to her was granted that she should be arrayed in fine linen, clean and white: for the fine linen is the righteousness of saints" we see his use of the word *byssinos*, which was actually what classical Greek people called, transparent linen: something that was worn very frequently by the ancient Egyptians, and classical Greeks and Romans. In the early messianic movement manifestly encouraging this wearing of fine spun linen they thereby demonstrated a kind of embodied eroticism, a sensual effrontery, indeed, a transfigured deviance (a theme that shall be returned to throughout this book as it is its underlying theme), that was as much a sexy act as it was a holy. This can be seen as all the more true in that it is very likely they wore no underwear in the early messianic movement and so were completely naked underneath.

Indeed, the light exhibitionism of not wearing underwear would have also been considered in those days a form of what we in our day would call Afrosensuality; even Barbara Watterson said it was practiced very often by the people of ancient Egypt when she exclaimed that the "Ancient Egyptian women wore their revealing dresses without much in the way of underwear". Moreover, the same could have also been said concerning the ancient Kushites. Even the ancient Hebrews would have performed various Afrosensual act-species, as can also be viewed by fathoming the depths of the Hebraic concept of *qodesh*, which meant holy, though mainly in the sexual sense of the word.

Effectively, the Hebraic words *qadesh* and *qadeshah* were, respectively, the male and female equivalents of refined one, holy disciple, and saint; and were also the equivalents of sexual one, shrine prostitute, and seducer. Basically, the holy men and holy women of the ancient Hebraic culture were like our modern Tantrics, understanding the spiritual value of their sexuality. And though the translators in the days of King James I translated the word *qadesh* as sodomite, such a mistranslation was an expression of the times. Its proper translation as sexual one helps us to understand why the only Scripture in the Bible to translate it as sodomite, Deuteronomy 23: 17, condemned its practice in Israel: due to the excessive practice of sexuality in Judea just before its fall, as can be read in Jeremiah. (As noted, most of the sexism and heterosexism we read in the Bible today came mainly from Renaissance and Reformation translators and not from the actual intentions of the early writers).

True, this idea of an Afrosensual early messianism may seem surprising, even spurious, to some readers; but that is only due to the modern Western mindset. We have been raised to view our bodies from a purely profane, even vulgar, perspective. However, there are other traces that can be discovered here in bodily performance and presentation. Indeed, this kind of embodied cultural performative was not lost on people like Frantz Fanon in their own consideration of the several colonial appropriations, and the decolonisation of the body. Fanon wrote, "The way people clothe themselves, together with the traditions of dress and finery that custom implies, constitutes the most distinctive form of a society's uniqueness, that is to say the one that is the most immediately perceptible. Within the general pattern of a given costume, there are of course always modifications of detail, innovations which in highly developed societies are the mark of fashion. But the effect as a whole remains homogeneous and great areas of civilization, immense cultural regions, can be grouped together on the basis of original, specific techniques of men's and women's dress."

Herein we see that control of clothing patterns, dress-codes, and sartorial fashions were more than just some patriarchal desires enforced by various religious leaders but a contribution to reaffirming a fractured identity. Fanon went on to say concerning the process of decolonising the body, "Tradition is no longer scoffed at by the group. The group no longer runs away from itself. The sense of the past is rediscovered, the worship of ancestors resumed…" Here, when the Messiah, the

Prophet, and the apostle Paul, set out to impose sartorial demarcations within their movements, it was not with the intent of controlling or delimiting female spatial and bodily expressions. What they were actually attempting to do was re-member their ancient signs of belonging and recognition, re-establish their traditional forms of cultural representation and manifestation, and re-appropriate those communal customs and practices that would be capable of decolonising both body and mind.

It is thereby, in the apostle Paul's understanding, for women to be bodily decolonised they also had to first be mentally decolonised. It is further, for this cause, that he wrote to the predominantly female messianic community of Philippi, saying: "Let this mind be in you, which was also in Christ Jesus: Who, being in the form of God, thought it not robbery to be equal with God: But made himself of no reputation, and took upon him the form of a servant, and was made in the likeness of men: And being found in fashion as a man, he humbled himself, and became obedient unto death, even the death of the cross." Essentially, what the apostle Paul was trying to say was that his female followers in Philippi should develop in themselves the same mind as the Messiah; and seek that better part that comes only from God. As the apostle Paul's main following among the Philippians was female I feel he saw this mentality as necessary to their bodily decolonisation.

It would be through these sorts of instances of bodily resistance that the act of maintaining one's own cultural practices and identity would become, in themselves, a performance of transfigured deviance. The apostle Paul therefore strategically wrote in his letter to Rome, the then seat of imperialism, "For as many as have sinned without law shall also perish without law: and as many as have sinned in the law shall be judged by the law; (For not the hearers of the law are just before God, but the doers of the law shall be justified. For when the Gentiles, which have not the law, do by nature the things contained in the law, these, having not the law, are a law unto themselves: Which shew the work of the law written in their hearts, their conscience also bearing witness, and their thoughts the mean while accusing or else excusing one another;) In the day when God shall judge the secrets of men by Jesus Christ according to my gospel" (Romans 2: 12-16). If we historicise and demystify this Scripture we can see that the apostle Paul, in this transfiguration of deviance, was through these remarks challenging all the political superstructures upon which Roman imperialism was built.

Still, it is my hope that you will not be too discouraged by this continual reference to transfiguration, particularly to that of the deviant, for, inasmuch as we all carry within us the Spirit and presence of Allah, we also manifest his divine nature, as it was written by the apostle Peter: "Whereby are given unto us exceeding great and precious promises: that by these you might be partakers of the divine nature, having escaped the corruption that is in the world through lust" (2Peter 1: 4). For the mystery of the divine nature was revealed when "Jesus answered them, Is it not written in your law, I said, Ye are gods? If he called them gods, unto whom the word of God came, and the scripture cannot be broken; Say ye of him, whom the Father hath sanctified and sent into the world, Thou blasphemest; because I said, I am the Son of God?"

Consequently, in the resurrecting of this kind of Black divinity we need to understand that there were in the ancient Egyptian traditions two chief gods of all: the sungod Ra and the nightgod Ausar. That which the West called worship of the sun or of the dead ancestors was, in actual fact, the honouring of these two concepts, respectively. Again, Hethor (who in ancient Egypt represented the goddess concept), in her form as the divine cow that carried and married Ra, represented both lover to Ra and mother and sister to Ausar and Auset. And being goddess of love, joy, pleasure, sex, dance, music, sensuality, wisdom, intelligence, and virtually every other good thing, Hethor also passed a lot of these attributes on to her daughter Auset.

It is from here that we are able to see how the resurrection of the father is in the son and of the mother is in the daughter. And as knowledge and sexuality both represented male and female divinity, respectively; so Ra and Hethor embodied these two concepts symbolically. For though Hethor was the second thing Tum created (the first being himself as Ra Atum), as the skygoddess Nut (who in ancient Egypt was the Nature concept) Hethor was mother, daughter, and lover to Ra. Yet this was not to justify incest – which was a lot less practiced in ancient Egypt than most Egyptologists appreciate – or any Oedipal ideas; but merely to represent the interconnection of the Black family. In similar vein, Ausar and Auset were the male and female equivalent of the ancient Egyptian concept of the Black: *Asr* and *Ast*. However, these words meant Black in a far more divine manifestation, as in Black god and Black goddess. Here they conveyed to the ancient Egyptians a sense of Black divinity, Black perfection, Black prosperity, Black beauty, Black sensuality, Black intelligence, Black strength, Black soul, Black magic, Black rapture, Black power, Black erotica, and Black love.

Black divinity, for both male and female, was nevertheless rooted in love, even the apostle Peter had this to say about it, "Seeing ye have purified your souls in obeying the truth through the Spirit unto unfeigned love of the brethren, see that ye love one another with a pure heart fervently: Being born again, not of corruptible seed, but of incorruptible, by the word of God" (1Peter 1: 22, 23). To which the apostle Paul also continued: "And though I have the gift of prophecy, and understand all mysteries, and all knowledge; and though I have all faith, so that I could remove mountains, and have no charity, I am nothing. And though I bestow all my goods to feed the poor, and though

I give my body to be burned, and have not charity, it profiteth me nothing. Charity suffereth long, and is kind"; and this charity he spoke of, being the Greek word *agape* (pronounced aw-gaw-pae) is thus our key to thearchism, and by extension, to divinity. It also manifests the Black divinity of the Black family, inasmuch as we all have suffered long and suffered hard.

True, we all are very familiar with that oft-quoted Scripture of the gospel of John, "For God so loved the world, that he gave his only begotten Son, *that whosoever believeth in him* should not perish, but have everlasting life" (John 3: 16; emphasis mine). Yet this kind of agapic message is a very similar message to one spoken in the Quran, "Say: *If you love Allah, follow me*: Allah will love you, and grant you protection from your sins. And Allah is Forgiving, Merciful" (Quran 3: 31; emphasis mine). The soteriology of these statements being undeniable, because Allah, who definitely loves us, also desires to boast over us; as was written, "And the Lord said unto Satan, Hast thou considered my servant Job, that there is none like him in the earth, a perfect and upright man, one that feareth God, and escheweth evil? and still he holdeth fast his integrity, although thou movedst me against him, to destroy him without cause" (Job 2: 3). Hereby, it is always necessary to remember the power of Allah, for he said again through his prophet Isaiah:

> *"Behold, I have created the smith that bloweth the coals in the fire, and that bringeth forth an instrument for his work; and I have created the waster to destroy." "When thou passest through the waters, I will be with thee; and through the rivers, they shall not overflow thee: when thou walkest through the fire, thou shalt not be burned; neither shall the flame kindle upon thee. For I am the Lord thy God, the Holy One of Israel, thy Saviour: I gave Egypt for thy ransom, Ethiopia and Seba for thee. Since thou wast precious in my sight, thou hast been honourable, and I have loved thee" (Isaiah 54: 16; 43: 2-4).*

The obvious question to ask at this point would be: what then is Allah's core essence? As we have already hinted at earlier, it could therefore be assumed that his essential nature is actually Romantic (*Ashiq*) or Erotic (*Shawq*). ... Though, it is true that such may not be false: yet to say his essence is Sexuality, Sensuality, or Eros is too hot, too emotive, and too affective. Then again, if we were to say that Allah's essential nature was actually Agapic (Rahman) or Empathic (Rahim); it is true that such also may not be false either. Truly, Allah's essence is Compassion, Benevolence, or Pathos, yet such a vision and perception of Allah is incomplete too. It is too cold, too thoughtful, and too nice. Such is like the brain and the heart. The two work together to fully integrate love into what I call the libido. In that sense, Allah's essence could be called Libidinal, or to use, again, the Arabic language Muhibb.

In this sense, libido (*habba*) proves to be greater than purity as any purity without libido leads to internal uncleanness or blind obedience. Libido proves to be greater than faith as any faith without libido breeds superstition, paranoia, and open idolatry. Libido proves to be greater than justice as any justice without libido leaves all of us sinners under the judgment of Allah. Libido proves to be greater than sensitivity as any sensitivity without libido lacks discipline, correction, and even honesty. Libido proves to be greater than wisdom as any wisdom without libido is trickery, deception, and delusional arrogance. Libido proves to be greater than truth as any truth without libido is a self-serving lie or a self-loathing fear. Libido proves to be greater than peace as any peace without libido is hypocritical, fake, and doomed to be broken. Libido further proves to be greater than grace as any grace without libido leads to weak self-oppression or vain self-righteousness. Libido even proves to be greater than hell as it can turn even the worst of hells into the most beautiful of heavens.

Undoubtedly, most Muslims will at this point question this particular perception of Allah. To these Muslims Allah has ninety-nine names and attributes, each used specifically by the Prophet in the Quran, and of all these names most Muslims have agreed, whether due to tradition or to the fear of going beyond tradition, or beyond all bounds, that the greatest name of God will always be Allah. The reason they give for this is that this name encompasses all the other names written in the Quran. However, this theory only ends up turning Allah into a pick and choose with regard to his true mentality. This name therefore basically answers every problem, becoming a tool to be used to promote or defend whatever cause we have. But ultimately this is putting a band aid on a broken arm. Allah needs a clear focus, central aim, and key definition. That is, Allah, like humanity, must have a clear intent, reason, meaning for being. If Allah works in mysterious ways, what is the aim, goal, and overall motivation that drives him?

For the record, this is based more so on my search to find Allah's essence or nature, because one thing we know for sure: Allah may change his covenant, he may change his laws, he may change his prophetic word, he may even change his mind. Indeed, it is said of Allah that he is both slow to anger and his wrath flares in an instant. However, the nature of Allah, his very essence, is without either change or variability. He is the same yesterday, today, and forever. So again, the essence of Allah is important. Saying the name Allah encompasses his entire being may sound good and well, but again it lacks focus. Consequently, Allah not only needs a focal point; a single dominant focus; but he needs it to outweigh all other foci, attributes, and names so thoroughly that the imbalance can be measured like the 80/20 scale. Here, it would more likely be that 20 percent of the names/attributes – though actually closer to one percent, as it is only one specific name – making up 80 percent of his personhood and personality, and within the Black thearchy this name/attribute is Muhibb/*habba*.

The concept and personhood of Muhibb is *the* central aspect of Black thearchism: conveying the essence of Allah as the Love Triad of the agapic, empathic, and erotic energy that permeates the universe inspiring and motivating all interactivity. Yet this does not contradict godbody theory, even though to most godbodies Allah is one, and we identify him as knowledge, science, or intelligence. Still, to us Allah manifests himself and discloses himself, not only through the sciences, or in fact through being the Grand Science, but by adding on to his knowledge so that it eventually becomes understanding.

Herein lies the genius of the godbody theory, we all say, believe, and appreciate that understanding is the greatest – and thereby the most important – we then take that a step further by acknowledging that the highest form of understanding is love. All Black thearchism does is it takes that a step further still, and say that the most refined form of love is libido (*habba*). Furthermore, to us, as understanding is the greatest, the greatest aspect and property of Allah, who is himself manifested as a Universal Intelligence, must thereby be none other than libido itself. Effectively, the greatest attribute and the most essential aspect of Allah is therefore libido.

Based on this definition of Allah at his essence, it is not impossible – indeed, it may even be commendable – for us Gods to acknowledge the Black woman's power and right to reach these same levels of Back divinity. Essentially, we Gods must learn to appreciate our Black women as Goddesses, as well as their souls, lest we forfeit our own divinity and the divinity of our people. In these sorts of areas we Black males have proven to be more religious than the religious, especially when it comes to what Allah said. While I may agree that we do need to become more dogmatic with regard to some things like our core ideology; I still say, we should try not to be too dogmatic about what Allah said while he was in the physical. Thereby we can embrace the general philosophy of what he tried to impart. There is actually a formula behind his philosophy and it applies just as much to women as it does to us Gods.

At the same time, one of the biggest bonuses that can come from us Gods actually considering Black women as Goddesses is that we will have effectively begun the process of transfiguring them. Transfiguration itself is a Tantric art that allows one to see their sexual partner as divine. Indeed, according to Tantric expert Dr. Ashby, "During Tantric training, each individual is instructed to regard the other as a divinity (which all humans are innately) and to worship each other as such and to alternate roles (each partner sees themselves as male or female) as they visualize the Life Force growing. During [any] 'physical' sexual intercourse between a man and a woman, it is the male who 'gives' and the female who 'receives'. Sexual intercourse [can accordingly, therefore, be] used to heighten the ecstatic feelings and to develop psychic energy for spiritual attainment." Not only so, but transfiguring Black women also psychologically conditions us to give her more pleasure during the sexual encounter, which in turn gives us a better reason than thinking of death or sad dogs or something ugly to prolong the sexual experience.

Moreover, as a result of these practices, we Black men can literally have multiple orgasms with the women we have thus transfigured. Indeed, by prolonging a sexual experience due to how amazing we think she is and how beautiful and divine we appreciate her to be, it is even possible, with time and practice, for us Black men to have literally hundreds of orgasms in our sexual encounters. Basically, by practicing what we in our day call "edging," we godbodies can experience heights of sexual ecstasy unimaginable. I can say myself, from my own experience: there actually comes a point in sexual congress when a man no longer wants, or even needs, to ejaculate as the level and extent of non-delusional ecstasy and pure sexual pleasure he has reached, through the simple process of transfiguring the Black woman into a Goddess.

In order to reach this state at will a man must, firstly, start practicing the art of letting the person he is having sex with enter *deep* into his heart through the process of transfiguration. Secondly, he must start practicing, for her sake, the self-discipline of not ejaculating. Such a practice is based on fully understanding the Tantric drive to attain a unification with the deity through sexual intimacy. Dr. Ashby further explained how in Tantric sexual experiences, "[The] participants are not allowed to reach climax ... in order to channel all energies towards concentrating on the goal: development of their Life Force and its union with the Transcendental – Absolute divine through ever increasing ecstasy and devotion ... Through repeated stimulation and concentration of the energies to the higher energy centers, the sublimation of the primal sexual and mental energy is possible."

From here it is also possible to understand the value and progress of what Tantric masters call: bindu sublimation. According to Swami Saraswati, a Tantric master in his own right, "Bindu means a point or a drop. ... The source of bindu is actually in the higher centres of the brain, but due to the development of emotions and passions, bindu falls down to the lower region where it is transformed into sperm and ova." It is this concept of bindu that contains the secret as to why "edging" is currently acknowledged in the West as a form of transcendental meditation. It keeps sexual energy at a highly charged and explosive state.

Moreover, as Swami Saraswati continued on, "According to tantra, the preservation of the bindu is absolutely necessary for two reasons. Firstly, the process of regeneration can only be carried out with the help of bindu. Secondly, all the spiritual experiences take place when there is an explosion of bindu. This explosion can result in the creation of a thought or of anything. Therefore, in tantra, certain practices are recommended by which the male partner can stop ejaculation and retain the bindu." At the same time, this is mainly encouraged, "not so much to preserve the semen, but because it causes a depression in the level of energy."

Thereby we can see and understand that the practice of prolonging the sexual experience (edging), keeps the sexual energy at peak levels and ultimately allows for maximum pleasure to be experienced by us male figures. The same is also true for the women, as Swami Saraswati further noted, "In the female body, the point of concentration is at mooladhara chakra, which is situated at the cervix, just behind the opening of the uterus. This is the point where space and time unite and explode in the form of an experience. In ordinary language of tantra it is called an awakening. In order to maintain the continuity of that experience, it is necessary for a build up of energy to take place at that particular bindu or point."

Essentially, by allowing a love object to enter into the inner chambers of our heart and take deep root, that is, by transfiguring them, we essentially give ourselves access to receiving multiple orgasms. Conversely, I also recognise how difficult it can be for us men, particularly us Black men, to open our hearts to anybody, let alone a romantic interest. There is an unspoken fear that any displays of vulnerability will lead to emasculation and future pain/trauma. There is also the obvious humiliation of being called by our friends, or even by our love objects themselves, a simp, a bitch, or a chump who all up in their feelings, i.e., too emotional. "Never let anyone in your heart or they will either break it, abuse it, or take your kindness for weakness," so they say.

Though I am somewhat sympathetic to this advice, and I get the reasoning behind it, as someone who famously opens his heart regularly, and also gets disappointed regularly, I can say: I have no desire to ever stop opening my heart regardless of the name calling or mistreatment. First of all, I am confident enough in my own manhood to not care about name calling. Second, the rewards I get from opening my heart far exceed any pain I may have to endure as a result. To be sure, I never open my heart easily, and if someone breaks it I will never trust them again, even if we stay friends afterward. But that whole Stoic, cold, and closed off shit is dead. If such a person confronted me and called me a chump, I would very likely say, "You probably right," but deep in my heart I would be feeling sorry for them; knowing that they are not only missing out on the beauties, wonders, and joys of an emotionally intimate relationship, but also missing out on the orgasmic pleasures of sheer ecstasy that can only be reached by opening your heart to a love object and transfiguring them into a deity.

That notwithstanding, it is only natural, after experiencing a few of these kinds of sexual encounters, especially when the amount of sexual orgasms reach into the double digits, for both parties to assume it will only ever improve from there. While I am not saying such is impossible, it is nonetheless definitely improbable. That means there *will* be days and moments that you orgasm back into the single digits, or even worse, ejaculate/discharge. Do not worry too much about that, it is just a matter of getting back to transfiguration. Further, so long as both the God and Goddess practice, both the transfiguration of their lover and the holding back of their sexual discharge, they can open themselves up, in time, to storing enough sexual energy to gain supersensory abilities, or what the Tantrics call *siddhis*. These abilities will, in turn, provide us with all the more reason to transfigure them and them with all the more reason to transfigure us, but I might be getting a bit ahead of myself.

All these are Tantric concepts that are taught within the Tantric arts. Conversely, Tantric training has three prominent schools of thought that share their basic disciplines: the dakshina marga, the vama marga, and the kaula marga. To further explain the traditions of these three schools Dr. Ashby expertly continued, saying, "The first path is the conservative mainline of Tantrism including mandala meditations and worship of the Divine in the form of the Mother Goddess. The second includes traditionally forbidden elements, especially sexual intercourse (with detachment and non-ejaculation). The third is practiced by the Kula sect and is equivalent to Kundalini Yoga (Serpent Power)."

Furthermore, to provide a greater clarification of these schools: First note, the dakshina marga is the right hand path. They teach a celibate, sensorial, devotional, and vegetarian lifestyle. Second, the vama marga is the left hand path. They teach polyamory, sorcery, sacrilegiousness, drunkenness, and eating meats (like beef). This path is not for the weak minded and is very dangerous for most people. It can even be related to mental illness if an unstable mind practices it. Finally, the kaula marga is the united path. They teach sexual, supersensorial, religious, pharmacological, and dietary union with the Creator and Creatrix (Shiva and Shakti). Having myself learned from the kaula school I will say their lessons on transfiguring the Black woman have improved my sex life dramatically.

Nevertheless Malcolm X also lost none of these idea when he considered the divine positioning of the Black woman. Indeed, his understanding was based more on the pathology (sickness) of Black men toward disparaging and disregarding Black women than showing them the love they deserve. We have not protected them, we have not cared for them, we have not honoured them; for this cause, Malcolm X basically felt that such behaviours would only produce for us a direct course to our own enfeeblement, "The Honorable Elijah Muhammad teaches us that the black man is going around saying he wants respect; well, the black man never will get anybody's respect until he first learns to respect his own woman! The black man needs *today* to stand up and throw off the weaknesses imposed upon him by the slavemaster white man! The black man needs to start today to shelter and protect and *respect* his black woman!" When we Gods can do this we will really reach that divine nature we understand to be our birthright.

Playing With the Cards We Were Dealt

With regard to the question of bond and free we find lurking beneath the surface, in both silenced and echoed voices, the obvious question of the enslaving of human bodies. This is where the apostle Paul *appears* to differ substantially from Malcolm X; but upon closer examination, the two are not that far apart. Although in the Scriptures the apostle Paul said: "Servants, be obedient to them that are your masters according to the flesh, with fear and trembling, in singleness of your heart, as unto Christ; Not with eyeservice, as menpleasers; but as the servants of Christ, doing the will of God from the heart; With good will doing service, as to the Lord, and not to men: Knowing that whatsoever good thing any man doeth, the same shall he receive of the Lord, whether he be bond or free." He also said, "And we beseech you, brethren, to know them which labour among you, and are over you in the Lord, and admonish you; And to esteem them very highly in love for their work's sake. And be at peace among yourselves."

The apostle Paul was not there encouraging slavery, he was actually encouraging work. The imminence of the kingdom of God to him was not cause enough to stop with their secular lives. Such a prescience for what became the Western work ethic, again, speaks volumes by its silences. Fanon in fact helps us uncover the hidden meanings and subtexts behind why the apostle Paul was so concerned with promoting and encouraging these anti-imperialist communities to maintain their secular jobs, positions, and class placements in society: "colonialism is not simply content to impose its rule upon the present and the future of the dominated country. Colonialism is not satisfied merely with holding a people in its grip and emptying the native's brain of all form and content. By a kind of perverted logic, it turns to the past of the oppressed people, and distorts, disfigures and destroys it."

Basically, what the apostle Paul was uncomfortably trying to do was negotiate being the leader of what, for all intents and purposes, was a subaltern movement of lowlifes, outlaws, bandits, thugs, revolutionaries, commoners, artisans, slaves, indentured workers, and women, with actually very few landowners, businessowners, and professionals. To be sure, according to all Roman records of the time, the first century messianic movement was a socially and publicly disreputable movement to belong to, on a par with being a member of a super-gang today. In this situation, the actions and act-species one used, not to mention the panoptical surveillance of the then imperial government, could determine life or death. He understood that his teachings either could be used as a vital resource for the community or get him executed for inflammatory and seditious speech.

The apostle Paul exemplified this uncomfortable tension in his second letter to the Thessalonian messianic communities, saying, "Now we command you, brethren, in the name of our Lord Jesus Christ, that ye withdraw yourselves from every brother that walketh disorderly, and not after the tradition which he received of us. For yourselves know how ye ought to follow us … For even when we were with you, this we commanded you, that if any would not work, neither should he eat." Again, although this message could theoretically be expressed as the apostle Paul's unceremonious attempt to organise the messianic movement into a class structure. It could, moreover, be asked from this if there is any idea more impressed upon a person than this within the current capitalist system?

To answer this question we must instead ask a new question: how would the apostle Paul feel about the work ethic within our capitalistic model? It is obvious that the apostle Paul had no intension of denying all non-workers the right to ever eat at all, but to make work itself a domain within which the anti-colonial and messianic struggles could also be fought. This strategic acculturation and amelioration of Paul's, what I call his "Anansian bargain," really came into sharp relief, especially in his letters to the messianic communities of Thessalonica, as can be seen when he wrote a little further down, "For we hear that there are some which walk among you disorderly, working not at all, but are busybodies. Now them that are such we command and exhort by our Lord Jesus Christ, that with quietness they work, and eat their own bread." Even emphasising this point in his first letter to them, saying, "And that ye study to be quiet, and to do your own business, and to work with your own hands, as we commanded you; That ye may walk honestly toward them that are without, and that ye may have lack of nothing."

Again, these kinds of statements are also familiar references within the prophetic tradition, where can be found statements such as, "These are the things that ye shall do; Speak ye every man the truth to his neighbour; execute the judgment of truth and peace in your gates: And let none of you imagine evil in your hearts against his neighbour; and love no false oath:" "Wash you, make you clean; put away the evil of your doings from before mine eyes; cease to do evil; Learn to do well; seek judgment, relieve the oppressed, judge the fatherless, plead for the widow." For the same Allah of ancient Hebraism and the same Allah of early messianism is the same Allah of social pragmatism. He even went on to say through his prophet Zechariah, "Thus speaketh the Lord of hosts, saying, Execute true judgment, and shew mercy and compassions every man to his brother: And oppress not the widow, nor the fatherless, the stranger, nor the poor; and let none of you imagine evil against his brother in your heart."

Thereby attempting to reveal justice and compassion to the earth; and to the widow and the fatherless, and the stranger and the poor, with a *completely partial* identification with them; and against the sinister hand of corrupting and oppressing individuals. All effectively highlighting Allah's determinative partiality towards certain subaltern groups, that the value, the "subterranean wealth" of these "worthless" groups, may not be absented from the record. Furthermore, the apostle Paul's Anansian bargain with the imperial state we should not assume to have been collusion, as he clearly had no problem with these subaltern groups among non-workers receiving daily bread and services from those who had the power to give. We know this because when he was given his commission from the other apostles; as he said later in a letter to the messianic communities of Galatia, "Only they would that we should remember the poor; the same which I also was forward to do." He even said to the Ephesian messianic communities, "Let him that stole steal no more: but rather let him labour, working with his hands the thing which is good, *that he may have to give to him that needeth*" (emphasis mine); thereby plainly showing his concern for the genuinely poor and needy, while still promoting a work ethic.

The defiant, indeed, deviant, bodies of God's people have throughout time been a message to the principalities and powers that have existed historically. Effectively, the expectation of social justice and ethics among the ancient Falashim was far more undeniable as their prophets fought and spoke against any oppressive or self-gratifying practices among the people. Yet during the time of the Neo-Persian Empire, the Falashim of the time colluded with imperialism thereby becoming rich through these same corrupted and oppressive practices. It is for this cause that Allah spoke to them through his prophet Malachi, saying, "And I will come near to you to judgment; and I will be a swift witness against the sorcerers, and against the adulterers, and against false swearers, and against those that oppress the hireling in his wages, the widow, and the fatherless, and that turn aside the stranger from his right, and fear not me, saith the Lord of hosts." In fact, in those days what marked out a prophet or the prophetic was this central theme: the calling of the people from the fear and worship of vanities and idols towards monism; that is, belief in the oneness of the family, the community, the society, the world, the environment, the universe, the astral, and the divine.

It is for this cause that the prophets cried out against destabilising actions like defrauding workers of their wages or oppressing strangers, the widow, and the fatherless; all practices continued in much sharper relief within modern Western societies, which have taken the mercantile mentality of the Near East and turned it into a moralised, indeed, a valorised, principle. But what did the prophet Amos have to say on this, "Hear this, O ye that swallow up the needy, even to make the poor of the land to fail, Saying, When will the new moon be gone, that we may sell corn? And the sabbath, that we may set forth wheat, making the ephah small, and the shekel great, and falsifying the balances by deceit? That we may buy the poor for silver, and the needy for a pair of shoes; yea, and sell the refuse of the wheat? The Lord hath sworn by the excellency of Jacob, Surely I will never forget any of their works." Again, this was written at a time when the Falashim were colluding with imperialism, only in this case it was the Syrian Empire.

Indeed, in late modernity these four groups would be called: the single parent and single parent families, foreign exiles, and the jobless non-workers. These four groups make up the current underclass, and have been the most marginalised class in all imperial geographies. These glaring inconsistencies in the imperial state eventually become clear to everybody, even as Fanon further informed us, "sooner or later, colonialism sees that it is not within its power to put into practice a project of economic and social reforms which will satisfy the aspirations of colonized people. Even where food supplies are concerned, colonialism gives proof of its inherent incapability. The colonialist state quickly discovers that if it wishes to disarm the nationalist parties on strictly economic questions then it will have to do in the colonies exactly what it has refused to do in its own country" (Fanon 1969: 166).

Moreover, it could be said, based on what we know of the apostle Paul's message, that he spoke directly against the vanity of placing your faith in good works, as he wrote to the messianic community of Rome, saying, "if Abraham were justified by works, he hath whereof to glory; but not before God. For what saith the scripture? Abraham believed God, and it was counted unto him for righteousness." (Romans 4: 2, 3). Nevertheless, this saying was written with the intention of building commitment and loyalty against passivity; not of abolishing the total practice of just works, let alone of those unto God; in the hopes of allowing the cultural reproduction of messianic practices as against Hebraic. Again, so as to show the subterranean representations he actually felt to be of importance he further explained that "by grace are ye saved through faith; and that not of yourselves: it is the gift of God: Not of works, lest any man should boast. For we are his workmanship, created in Christ Jesus *unto good works*, which God hath before ordained that we should walk in them" (emphasis mine).

However, Malcolm X was also in agreement concerning the work ethic, saying, "No Muslim who followed Elijah Muhammad could dance, gamble, date, attend movies, or sports, or take long vacations from work. Muslims slept no more than health required. Any domestic quarreling, any discourtesy, especially to women, was not allowed. No lying or stealing, and no insubordination to civil authority, except on the grounds of religious obligation." As the American Black people of his days were lost in a sea of confusion having no means of achieving success in a world designed against them. Malcolm X felt that these struggling Black people just needed to learn the right course. It is for this cause, he further continued, "The America Black man should be focusing his every effort toward building his own businesses, and decent homes for himself. As other ethnic groups have done, let the black people, wherever possible, however possible, patronize their own kind, hire their own kind, and start in those ways to build up the black race's ability to do for itself."

The obvious correlation here between these hopes and work ethics in the Nation of Islam and the apostle Paul's conviction that those claiming to be in the kingdom of God should admire those guided by their own work ethic is intriguing. In the late modern era, however, it is a very different story. Here it is political ideologues who fight for such ideals. Among them Rosa Luxemburg felt particularly compelled to promote these kinds of issues, stating, "A general requirement to work for all who are able to do so, from which small children, the aged and sick are exempted, is a matter of course in a socialist economy", but still, "The public at large must provide forthwith for those unable to work — not like now with paltry alms but with generous provision, socialized child-raising, enjoyable care for the elderly, public health care for the sick, etc." This general requirement to work, being not too dissimilar from the apostle Paul's and Malcolm X's work ethics, shows that the idea of people having to work is not simply a religious ideal but existed within a Leftist framework too.

This work ethic is and will also be necessary within godbodyism too, as to us work is itself a battleground through which we decolonise our minds and bodies. We must also encourage each other to make a reasonable contribution to our societies and our communities and thereby work for their improvement. For the grace manifested by Allah to the sinner is of his own doing, in that he loves them and desires to save them. Moreover, as the apostle Paul continued in his letter to the messianic communities of Rome, "What then? shall we sin, because we are not under the law, but under grace? God forbid. Know ye not, that to whom ye yield yourselves servants to obey, his servants ye are to whom ye obey; whether of sin unto death, or of obedience unto righteousness?" (Romans 6: 15, 16).

This statement takes on even newer bounds when one replaces the apostle Paul's use of the word sin with the word crime – which is how the first century readers would have interpreted it. However, when he used the word righteousness, the apostle Paul was here speaking specifically of the righteousness of Allah, and not that of colonial legality nor based on the standards of colonial legality. So if thereby the apostle Paul understood that Allah, in his righteousness, could judge as criminal that which he deemed to be criminal according to his own ethical interpretation, then the apostle Paul clearly saw him as all the more able to redeem from the colonial standards of criminality those whom he found to be of genuine spirit.

Malcolm X also agreed with such a sentiment, feeling himself that, in like manner, the Nation of Islam should be, and had to be, the agglomeration of Black people into a creditable community. "Our businesses sought to demonstrate to Black people what black people could do for themselves – if they would only unite, trade with each other – exclusively where possible – and hire each other, and in so doing, keep black money within the black communities, just as other minorities did." These Black communities, formulated as an expression not of instinctual aggression, self-interest, or some internal need for conquest and power; but in response to the depreciation of the Black population in the United States, were to uplift the people and allow us to become a decolonised race.

As to the apostle Paul's social theory for the colonised people of his time, it did bear some similarities to these, but his vision was primarily for the messianic communities to take care of themselves. His statement to the messianic communities of Corinth articulates this idea, "Who goeth a warfare any time at his own charges? who planteth a vineyard, and eateth not of the fruit thereof? … he that ploweth should plow in hope; … he that thresheth in hope should be partaker of his hope. If we have sown unto you spiritual things, is it a great thing if we shall reap your carnal things?" Here the apostle Paul was stating very plainly that the early messianic movement, which was still at the time predominantly a Black movement, should take care of its own. He was also showing and proving, like Malcolm X, that it was quite respectable for the people of God to provide for their own ministers instead of waiting on some other people to provide for them. And one thing is definitely sure, if the messianic movement raised any funds, those funds were reaped and shared out only among the brothers and sisters.

Effectively, the apostle Paul spoke all his arguments in favour of workers not in favour of capitalistic non-workers. We can see this by the statement following, "Now to him that worketh is the reward not reckoned of grace, but of debt." Here showing that when somebody works they deserve to reap the benefits thereof. Then again, we must not forget some of the more feudalistic ideas he espoused in the above, "who planteth a vineyard, and eateth not of the fruit thereof?" Surely, it was the capitalists and the feudal lords who owned the vineyard and the workers who merely worked it?

When the apostle Paul said, "he that ploweth should plow in hope;" he was saying in essence that the worker, the one who worked the plow, should receive of what he had worked. The feudal lord was not considered for as he said in a letter to Timothy, "The husbandman that *laboureth* must be first partaker of the fruits" (emphasis mine). I see the apostle Paul as talking here about those who plant *and* work the vineyard, because somewhere else he said "every man shall bear his own burden." So he was essentially saying that the person who works the vineyard is worthy of its fruits.

The importunity of the initial question also opens up a general insistence by the preachers of prosperity: there is a seed time and a harvest time. Those who wish to harvest must sow the right seeds. One who sows into financial success through their tithes and offerings will reap financial success in their lives and businesses. This is an obvious vulgarisation of what the apostle Paul said to the messianic communities of Galatia, "Be not deceived; God is not mocked: for whatsoever a man soweth, that shall he also reap." The trouble is these preachers fail to read further on, where it says; "For he that soweth to his flesh shall of the flesh reap corruption; but he that soweth to the Spirit shall of the Spirit reap life everlasting."

Even so, the apostle Paul said regarding his struggles to decolonise minds and bodies in the imperial underclass, that "we have this treasure in earthen vessels, that the excellency of the power may be of God, and not of us. We are troubled on every side, yet not distressed; we are perplexed, but not in despair; Persecuted, but not forsaken; cast down, but not destroyed; Always bearing about in the body the dying of the Lord Jesus, that the life also of Jesus might be made manifest in our body." Furthermore, as these inter-embodied interactions and confrontations transpired they would cause colonialists' spaces, and thereby the colonialists' right to power, to be problematised. Such problematisations even potentially triggering rebellion and sparking revolution.

What we see therefore is as Fanon also said, "Decolonization is the meeting of two forces, opposed to each other by their very nature, which results from and is nourished by the situation in the colonies. Their first encounter was marked by violence and their existence together – that is to say the exploitation of the native by the settler – was carried on by dint of a great array of bayonets and cannon." For this cause, the apostle Paul wrote again to the messianic communities of Rome, saying, "There is therefore now no condemnation to them which are in Christ Jesus, who walk not after the flesh, but after the Spirit. For the law of the Spirit of life in Christ Jesus hath made me free from the law of sin and death. For what the law could not do, in that it was weak through the flesh, God sending his own Son in the likeness of sinful flesh, and for sin, condemned sin in the flesh: That the righteousness of the law might be fulfilled in us, who walk not after the flesh, but after the Spirit." (Romans 8: 1-4). Again, while the Spirit hereby frees us from the legal requirement, according to the gospel the apostle Paul taught, it still does not free us completely from the responsibility to do righteous works; for we find the prophet Ezekiel crying out for Allah:

"Therefore, thou son of man, say unto the children of thy people, The righteousness of the righteous shall not deliver him in the day of his transgression: as for the wickedness of the wicked, he shall not fall thereby in the day that he turneth from his wickedness; neither shall the righteous be able to live for his righteousness in the day that he sinneth. When I shall say to the righteous, that he shall surely live; if he trust to his own righteousness, and commit iniquity, all his righteousness shall not be remembered; but for his iniquity that he hath committed, he shall die for it. Again, when I say unto the wicked, Thou shalt surely die; if he turn from his sin, and do that which is lawful and right; If the wicked restore the pledge, give again that he had robbed, walk in the statutes of life, without committing iniquity; he shall surely live, he shall not die. None of his sins that he hath committed shall be mentioned unto him: he hath done that which is lawful and right; he shall surely live. Yet the children of thy people say, The way of the Lord is not equal: but as for them, their way is not equal" (Ezekiel 33: 12-17).

This form of justice and ethics, this very realistic form of justice and ethics; is Allah's form of justice and ethics. That Allah held justice and righteousness as so essential effectively showed that Allah himself was and is beyond anything we have thus far assumed of him. Still, as we know, modern Western society has no formal conception of ethical orientation. Modernity sees justice and ethics purely in the liberal and in the popular. In fact, popular opinion is the main standard of justice and ethics in most modern societies. Here it is society that keeps itself from its own redemption, but we poor righteous teachers, taking our stand, will ultimately bring to society a powerful liberation through our own iron determination.

Pulling the Race Card and other Absurdities

The final social field of contest we shall consider in relation to the apostle Paul here is race. It is here that the apostle Paul is unfortunately usually believed to be anti-Semitic and bigoted. However, as he wrote again in his letter to the messianic communities of Rome, "For I could wish that myself were accursed from Christ for my brethren, my kinsmen according to the flesh: Who are Israelites; to whom pertaineth the adoption, and the glory, and the covenants, and the giving of the law, and the service of God, and the promises; Whose are the fathers, and of whom as concerning the flesh Christ came, who is over all, God blessed for ever. Amen" (Romans 9: 3-5). Malcolm X also saw this kind of divine calling on the Black people of his time, saying, "We believe that the miserable plight of America's twenty million black people is the fulfillment of divine prophecy. We also believe the presence today in America of The Honorable Elijah Muhammad, his teachings among the so-called Negroes, and his naked warning to America concerning her treatment of these so-called Negroes, is all the fulfillment of divine prophecy."

We Black people of the world have historically been lost in a system designed against us. Here Fanon, in his own attempts to encourage the decolonisation of mind and body, articulated what we could take to be a new prospect for us struggling Black people to aspire to, reminding us how "decolonization is quite simply the replacing of certain 'species' of men [and women] by [other] 'species' of men [and women]. Without any period of transition, there is a total, complete and absolute substitution." The apostle Paul's revolutionary theory also contained certain similarities, as he wrote to the messianic fellowships of Corinth, "Therefore if any man be in Christ, he is a new creature: old things are passed away; behold, all things are become new. And all things are of God, who hath reconciled us to himself by Jesus Christ, and hath given to us the ministry of reconciliation. To wit, that God was in Christ, reconciling the world unto himself, not imputing their trespasses unto them; and hath committed unto us the word of reconciliation. Now then we are ambassadors for Christ, as though God did beseech you by us: we pray you in Christ's stead, be ye reconciled to God" (2Corinthians 5: 17-20).

This Scripture contains herein something of the elemental, the environmental, even the primal, about it. Whereas with Fanon the new humanity comes about by armed struggle and resistance, with the apostle Paul the new creature comes about by accepting the Lordship and Messiahship of Jesus. Indeed, the Black thearchy posits the idea that every creature in the universe, animate and inanimate, is entitled to give and receive love, peace, and happiness in life, for as long as they shall live. These rights should also be protected by the Gods and Goddesses of their various jurisdictions, to the beautifying of the creation. Now while such an ask may seem innocent enough in our current world of decoupled Church from State, in the first century by identifying the representatives of the imperial government, and particularly the Caesar himself, as possessing the divine right to make, break, and judge the law as they saw fit, the people of society effectively avoided persecution from that very same imperial government.

Still, even though he only saw himself as an ambassador for the Messiah, the apostle Paul's own messianism was fundamentally one of political significance: "For we wrestle not against flesh and blood, but against principalities, against powers, against the rulers of the darkness of this world, against spiritual wickedness in high places." In this Scripture – which is usually taken for an otherworldly warfare – can be apprehended within its historical absences voices silenced yet historicised and embodied. The first thing we can identify is that a principality was considered any territory ruled over by a prince. The next thing we can identify is that the Greek word used here for powers was not *dynamis,* but was in fact the word *exousia,* which meant jurisdiction. Now, these two concepts possess spatiality, territoriality, and historicity. Again, the word used for world was cosmos, which can translate to world, universe, or even to system. Herein, the apostle Paul was stating that this dark system of socio-political governments and jurisdictions, and all their spiritual wickedness, was to be the messianic movement's true enemy and opponent.

Furthermore, the apostle Paul also explained how we were to fight against these enemies and opponents, stating, "For though we walk in the flesh, we do not war after the flesh: (For the weapons of our warfare are not carnal, but mighty through God to the pulling down of strong holds;) Casting down imaginations, and every high thing that exalteth itself against the knowledge of God, and bringing into captivity every thought to the obedience of Christ" (2Corinthians 10: 4, 5). Again, the word used here for imaginations was the word *logismos,* literally meaning logic or reasoning. The apostle Paul was basically encouraging his followers to cast down the vain logic of colonial princes and authorities, or said another way, cast down the vain ideology of imperialism. Here, debate was to be the central methodology the apostle Paul was encouraging. To him the messianic movement was to represent an ethical entity so righteous that it put the Roman Empire to shame.

To explain this methodology for pulling down logical and psychological strongholds, the apostle Paul said, "Beware lest any man spoil you through philosophy and vain deceit, after the tradition of men, after the rudiments of the world, and not after Christ. For in him dwelleth all the fulness of the Godhead bodily." But what made the messianic event so significant, at least to the apostle Paul? We actually get a glimpse of it as he continues on in this letter to the messianic communities of Colossae: "Blotting out the handwriting of ordinances that was against us, which was contrary to us, and took it out of the way, nailing it to his cross; And having spoiled principalities and powers, he made a shew of them openly, triumphing over them in it." While the apostle Paul was clearly speaking here about the laws of Moses, there was nonetheless, hidden in what was being silenced, a subterranean voice, whispered and absented, that we can detect through the prism of the apostle Paul's over-surveilled body, and his over-cautiousness due to his consciousness of that over-surveillance.

The apostle Paul's rhetoric calls for, demands, de-mystification; through which can be glimpsed the apostle Paul's antinomian, even anarchic, leanings. These leanings will have to be explored more fully later on, but for now simply acknowledge that the apostle Paul saw the goal of reconciling the world to Allah as more than merely a continuum of religious or spiritual act-species, he saw it as political, even as world historical. Herein, the apostle Paul was not blind to the suffering of his own race but sought all the more for their unification to Allah, saying, "Brethren, my heart's desire and prayer to God for Israel is, that they might be saved. For I bear them record that they have a zeal of God, but not according to knowledge" (Romans 10: 1, 2), which he wrote, again, to the messianic communities of Rome. Malcolm X also saw lack of knowledge in the Black communities of America as our greatest weakness, saying, "My homemade education gave me, with every additional book that I read, a little bit more sensitivity to the deafness, dumbness and blindness that was afflicting the black race in America."

Through this prism we can also see that what the apostle Paul was most likely trying to explain in all these verses was that through the understanding that he received from Allah he could see that what the state-sponsored lynching of the Messiah on the cross ultimately did was render the state utterly impotent, thereby removing all moral and ethical credibility from the Roman government. The injustice of the Messiah's death effectively exposed the Roman state implied in the conception of "pax Romana" instead as "violence incarnate," with no intention of bringing peace, protection, prosperity, or pride to the colonised masses, or subject nations.

As Fanon also said concerning colonial states, their only intention is to subjugate them and to break them. Yet, even though, "In the colonial context the settler only ends his work of breaking in the native when the latter admits loudly and intelligibly the supremacy of the white man's values. In the period of decolonization, the colonized masses mock at these very values, insult them and vomit them up." This is telling, as the apostle Paul, at least in his beginnings, and very likely for all his adult life, valued his Roman citizenship. Indeed, there is almost a hint of pride that passes through the ages and pages of time and sources when one reads Paul saying to the chief captain sent in to quiet a riot that was happening, "I was free born" (Acts 22: 28). Though these kinds of contradictions are not uncommon in freedom fighters and revolutionaries they are also telling in there uncomfortable absurdity.

Any Anansian negotiations on the part of the freedom fighter, any transfigured deviances in the social spheres of conflict, these Malcolm X considered to be merely birthing pangs as a result of a liberation struggle. Fanon had a similar understanding of the mass element, seeing the liberation struggle occurring in two phases. Of these, he recognised that it is "during the second period, which is characterized by the putting into operation of the enemy offensive. The colonial forces, once the explosion has taken place, regroup and reorganize, inaugurating methods of warfare which correspond to the nature of the rising. This offensive will call in question the ideal, Utopian atmosphere of the first phase. The enemy attacks, and concentrates large forces on certain definitive points. The local group is quickly overrun, all the more so because it tends to seek the forefront of the battle. ... But the losses are serious, and doubts spring up and begin to weigh heavily upon the rebels. [Here, the] group faces a local attack as if it were a decisive test."

These stages of systemic decolonisation, after decolonisation has occurred in mind and body, then it is about putting it into effect in the society. When this process begins the colonial regime will obviously declare all participants illegal, criminal, deviant, even seditious, and will thereby feel within their rights to prosecute or even execute all perpetrators. This may be true, but as Fanon further pointed out, "The oppressor's government can set up commissions of inquiry and of information daily if it wants to; in the eyes of the native, these commissions do not exist. The fact is that soon we shall have had seven years of crimes in Algeria and there has not yet been a single Frenchmen indicted before a French court of justice for the murder of an Algerian. In Indo-China, in Madagascar or in the colonies the native has always known that he need expect nothing from the other side. ... On the logical plane, the Manichaeism of the settler produces a Manichaeism of the native. To the theory of the 'absolute evil of the native' the theory of the 'absolute evil of the settler' replies."

It may feel strange to consider, but as Black people in the world today most of our minds, bodies, and cultures are deviant to White people, indeed, they are devilish. In this, Black divinity inverts the White gaze and imposes on it a counter-gaze; inverts their discourse and imposes on it a counter-discourse; inverts their narrative and imposes on it a counter-narrative; inverts their culture and imposes on it a counter-culture; and inverts their performances and imposes on them counter-performances. If to White people Black people must be the devil, then to Black people White people will also be the devil. If White people really believe they are a chosen or divine race, then Black people will counter that with a belief in our own divinity as a race. If, "in fact, my life is worth as much as the settler's, his glance no longer turns me into stone. I am no longer on tenderhooks in his presence; in fact, I don't give a damn for him."

Now let us not forget that Malcolm X was himself good friends with Frantz Fanon, who was himself a key figure in the Algerian Revolution; and was also friends with Ali Shari'ati, a key figure in the Iranian Revolution; and with Fidel Castro, the key figure in the Cuban Revolution; and with Kwame Nkrumah, the key figure in the Ghanaian Revolution; and with Patrice Lumumba, the key figure in the Congolese Revolution; and also travelled to Africa and Asia long before he left the Nation of Islam. As he went on himself to say, "[There was great] national publicity ... in the offing for the Nation of Islam [so] Mr Muhammad sent me on a three-week trip to Africa. Even as small as we then were, some of the African and Asian personages had sent Mr Muhammad private word that they liked his efforts to awaken and lift up the American black people. Sometimes, the messages had been sent through me. As Mr Muhammad's emissary, I went to Egypt, *Arabia*, to the Sudan, to Nigeria, and Ghana" (Malcolm X 2001: 339; emphasis mine).

Herein, the Elijah's method for decolonising the Black American mind and body, and all neo-colonialist spaces, real or imagined (that is, the public and semi-public locations where the spatial representation of neo-colonial power existed: indeed, the geography of domination); was to contest these sites of inter-embodied confrontation. Malcolm X also went on to note how, "[If an] addict is brought into the local Muslim restaurant, he may occasionally be exposed to some other social situations – among proud, clean Muslims who show each other mutual affection and respect instead of the familiar hostility of the ghetto streets. For the first time in years, the addict [will hear] himself called, genuinely, 'Brother', 'Sir' and 'Mr'." And, "That's a powerful combination for a man who has been existing in the mud of society."

In like manner the apostle Paul wrote to the messianic communities of Rome, "For I speak to you Gentiles, inasmuch as I am the apostle of the Gentiles, I magnify mine office: If by any means I may provoke to emulation them which are my flesh, and might save some of them. For if the casting away of them be the reconciling of the world, what shall the receiving of them be, but life from the dead?" (Romans 11: 13-15). Here, in declaring himself an apostle to the Gentiles (in Greek *ethnos*, meaning nations), the apostle Paul was literally identifying himself as the anti-racist *par excellence*. However, in saying that his message to the nations (*ethnos*) was for the purpose of stirring up his own Falashim people (Parashim, from where we get the word Pharisees, which meant set apart ones, consecrated ones, or separatists, was a corruption of the Ethiopic Falashim, which meant wanderer, nomad, or stranger – a culture very suited for a tentmaker) towards godliness by emulation, he could also be perceived to be justifying rivalry and competition. So what about competition?

It could be said at this point, surely, the apostle Paul viewed competition as a legitimate form of self-expression and self-identification, for he said, "And every man that striveth for the mastery is temperate in all things. Now they do it to obtain a corruptible crown; but we an incorruptible"? If the apostle Paul did not problematise competitive striving then why should we start doing so now? The answer, however, is that mental or bodily identification with competitiveness leads inexorably to carnality, even as the apostle Paul said again, "For ye are yet carnal: for whereas there is among you envying, and strife, and divisions, are ye not carnal, and walk as men?" Indeed, he also encouraged his followers in Galatia, saying, "If we live in the Spirit, let us also walk in the Spirit. Let us not be desirous of vain glory, provoking one another, envying one another." Again, he further wrote to the messianic communities of Corinth, saying, "God hath chosen the foolish things of the world to confound the wise; and God hath chosen the weak things of the world to confound the things which are mighty; And base things of the world, and things which are despised, hath God chosen, yea, and things which are not, to bring to nought things that are: That no flesh should glory in his presence" (1Corinthians 1: 27-29).

Effectively, while the apostle Paul admitted that he saw the purpose of his mission to the nations to be to provoke his own people to jealousy, such was not done to inspire competetiveness, so as to lead them to glory in their own righteousness, but based on an understanding that all living creatures learn by osmosis and emulation, and without seeing an incorruptible people how could his own people possibly learn to be incorruptible? It is here that the apostle Paul proved himself a true product of the world of Roman imperialism. But, whereas among most of the Falashim Judeans of his time the methodology of seditious militarism and armed insurrectionism were the chosen forms of bodily counter-performance against the Roman Empire, the apostle Paul incorporated a more socially viable form of engagement with Roman imperialism, based on re-educating and re-unifying the masses throughout the Roman world.

Using his own field of expertise, the nineteenth century Russian geographer and social scientist, Pyotr Kropotkin, speaking on Darwin's *The Descent of Man* also articulated how:

"He [further] pointed out how, in numberless animal societies, the struggle [of existence] is replaced by co-operation, and how that substitution results in the development of intellectual and moral faculties which secure to the species the best conditions for survival. He intimated that in such cases the fittest are not the physically strongest, nor the cunningest, but those who learn to combine so as mutually to support each other, strong and weak alike, for the welfare of the community."

This idea was also maintained in what could be considered a summary of Kropotkin's views of a human historiography of competition, "It is evident that it would be quite contrary to all that we know of nature ... if a creature so defenceless as man was at his beginnings should have found his protection and his way to progress, not in mutual support, like other animals, but in a reckless competition for personal advantages, with no regard to the interests of the species. To a mind accustomed to the idea of unity in nature, such a proposition appears utterly indefensible." Moreover, "Sociability and need of mutual aid and support are such inherent parts of human nature that at no time of history can we discover men living in small isolated families, fighting each other for the means of subsistence. On the contrary, modern research ... proves that since the very beginning of their prehistoric life men used to agglomerate into *gentes*, clans, or tribes, maintained by an idea of common descent and by worship of common ancestors."

Moreover, this idea of a co-operative, re-unification process was witnessed by Fanon in the adoption by the Black people of his time of the philosophy of what we in the Anglophone countries would call Negroism. He identified that, "This rush of Negro-ism against the white man's contempt showed itself in certain spheres to be the one idea capable of lifting interdictions and anathemas. Because the New Guinean or Kenyan intellectuals found themselves above all up against a general ostracism and delivered to the combined contempt of their overlords, their reaction was to sing praises in admiration of each other." Yet he could not, at the same time, fail to notice a contradiction. In spite of these intellectuals' praising and honouring their Black identity, they were still beholden to the system, the objective reality, of colonial morality and legality. "In Kenya, for example, during the Mau-Mau rebellion, not a single well-known nationalist declared his affiliation with the movement, or even tried to defend the men involved in it" (Fanon 1969: 171).

These kinds of contradictions did not elude the apostle Paul either, therefore, though his doctrine concerning the Gentiles (*ethnos*) may have been somewhat more lenient than his doctrine concerning his own Falashim people, such was not the same with regard to his doctrine concerning the elites within the movement, as we can see in his letter to the evangelist Timothy, "Charge them that are rich in this world, that they be not highminded, nor trust in uncertain riches, but in the living God, who giveth us richly all things to enjoy; That they do good, that they be rich in good works, ready to distribute, willing to communicate; Laying up in store for themselves a good foundation against the time to come" (1Timothy 6: 17-19). Malcolm X also had no tolerance, in his time, for the concept of a Black bourgeoisie (pronounced boo-jwa-zee), as he said "it is those few bourgeois Negroes, rushing to throw away their little money in the white man's luxury hotels, his swanky nightclubs, and big, fine, exclusive restaurants … proving they're integrated." Such concerns were obviously far from Malcolm X.

Even Frantz Fanon stood up against what he would go on to call the "Negro bourgeoisie," believing himself only in the concept of decolonisation, saying, "This bourgeoisie, expressing its mediocrity in its profits, its achievements and in its thought, tries to hide this mediocrity by buildings which have prestige value at the individual level, by chromium plating on big American cars, by holidays on the Riviera and week-ends in neon-lit night-clubs." Yet Fanon was not here speaking against wealth in general or even the right to wealth. To calm his critics Fanon further explained concerning what could happen during the process of a political decolonisation, "The former colonial power increases its demands, accumulates concessions and guarantees and takes fewer and fewer pains to mask the hold it has over the national government. The people stagnate deplorably in unbearable poverty; slowly they awaken to the unutterable treason of their leaders. This awakening is all the more acute in that the bourgeoisie is incapable of learning its lesson. … [This] bourgeois caste, that section of the nation which annexes for its own profit all the wealth of the country, by a kind of unexpected logic will pass disparaging judgements upon the other Negroes and the other Arabs that more often than not are reminiscent of the racist doctrines of the former representatives of the colonial power."

From here Malcolm X saw the problem faced by the Black community. Thereby he desperately sought to remind his people, "There are two types of Negroes in this country. There's the bourgeois type who blinds himself to the condition of his people, and who is satisfied with token solutions. He's in the minority. He's a handful. He's usually the handpicked Negro who benefits from token integration." See, "Most of the so-called Negroes that you listen to on the race problem usually … are Negroes who have been put in that position by the white man himself. And when they speak they're not speaking for black people, they're saying exactly what they know the white man who put them in that position wants to hear them say." The social disintegration produced as a result of social forces beyond the control of the various Black leaders thereby has the potential to expose the true persona of those who purport to speak for us.

Herein, Malcolm X was very forthright. He said concerning the Black predicament of 1960s America, "you have two types of Negro. The old type and the new type. Most of you know the old type. When you read about him in history during slavery he was called 'Uncle Tom.' He was the house Negro. And during slavery you had two Negroes. You had the house Negro and the field Negro. The house Negro usually lived close to his master. He dressed like his master. He wore his master's second-hand clothes. He ate food that his master left on the table. And he lived in his master's house – probably in the basement or the attic – but he still lived in the master's house. So whenever that house Negro identified himself, he always identified himself in the same sense that his master identified himself." The example given by Malcolm X of this pathology is, "When the master would be sick, the house Negro identified himself so much with his master he'd say, 'What's the matter boss, we sick? His master's pain was his pain."

Clearly, the stand-up call to fight for liberation with a willingness to use violence if necessary is a truly noble and efficacious pursuit for any enslaved people. Here Malcolm X noted the second class of Negro during the time of slavery. "But then you had another Negro out in the field. The house Negro was in the minority … the field Negroes were the masses. They were in the majority. When the master got sick, they prayed that he'd die." Indeed, "If someone came to the house Negro and said, 'Let's go, let's separate,' naturally that Uncle Tom would say, 'Go where? What could I do without boss? Where would I live? How would I dress? Who would look out for me?' That's the house Negro. But if you went to the field Negro and said, 'Let's go, let's separate,' he wouldn't even ask you where or how. He'd say, 'Yes, let's go.'"

Fanon and Malcolm X were effectively seeking for the general improvement of their people, not for the creation of an elite among their people. Yet it could still be asked, where did the apostle Paul's heart lie in his own racial programme? Firstly, concerning the leaders in our community becoming elite or receiving a large amount of money for preaching the gospel, the apostle Paul does say you should give to preachers of the word, acknowledging, "Now ye Philippians know also, that in the beginning of the gospel, when I departed from Macedonia, no church communicated with me as concerning giving and receiving, but ye only. For even in Thessalonica ye sent once and again unto my necessity." So the apostle Paul felt that revolution leaders were worthy of pay, as any and all workers are worthy of pay.

There is nothing wrong with leaders receiving payment for administering leadership, but there are some who would prey on the gullible so as to beguile them out of their money. The apostle Paul said of such people they are lost, drowned in the "Perverse disputing of men of corrupt minds, and destitute of the truth, supposing that gain is godliness". To the apostle Paul godliness was not found in a measure of financial gain. Godliness was found in living by righteousness. How can working and underclass people possibly sow their way out of financial difficulty without any capital or assets of their own to sow into? God blesses what you have, but if you have no assets or capital then where will your blessing go?

Still, perhaps the most powerful argument most prosperity preachers use is this Scripture oft-quoted by them, "For ye know the grace of our Lord Jesus Christ, that, though he was rich, yet for your sakes he became poor, that ye through his poverty might be rich." What makes this Scripture so complicated is the fact that we know most of the people in the early messianic movement were poor. Whether he was talking about spiritual wealth or material we do not know for sure, but it is more likely, considering the context in which it was written, that he was talking about material. So, was this statement a bold-faced assertion by the apostle Paul in defence of material prosperity, and if so of a capitalist standard and capitalist class?

In order to grasp fully what the apostle Paul was trying to convey let us look at the verses preceding this one to make sense of its context. The apostle Paul said here, in his second letter to Corinth, "Moreover, brethren, we do you to wit of the grace of God bestowed on the churches of Macedonia; How that in a great trial of affliction the abundance of their joy and their deep poverty abounded unto the riches of their liberality." The apostle Paul was speaking here of the messianic communities of Macedon, which included Philippi, Berea, and Thessalonica. Although they were poor materially, and even in extreme poverty, they gave liberally to the apostle Paul. But why was he bringing this up? Because he wanted them to give liberally too, when Titus came to them.

The apostle Paul continued in the next verses of the same chapter, "Therefore, as ye abound in every thing, in faith, and utterance, and knowledge, and in all diligence, and in your love to us, see that ye abound in this grace also. I speak not by commandment, but by occasion of the forwardness of others, and to prove the sincerity of your love." But as we continue on we can find the true social opinions of the apostle Paul staring us right in the face: "For I mean not that other men be eased, and ye burdened: But by an equality, that now at this time your abundance may be a supply for their want, that their abundance also may be a supply for your want: that there may be an equality: As it is written, He that had gathered much had nothing over; and he that had gathered little had no lack." So that now we can see in a nutshell the apostle Paul's social philosophy, which absolutely rubbishes the capitalist philosophy. Furthermore, we see here the apostle Paul stating very plainly his desire for economic equality, and even using the Torah to back it up.

That is not to say that the apostle Paul necessarily sided with Roman economic policy. Evidently, he was not the biggest fan of how things operated throughout most of the empire. We can see this by the succeeding statement he made to the evangelist

Timothy, "But they that will be rich fall into temptation and a snare, and into many foolish and hurtful lusts, which drown men in destruction and perdition." So again, what would the apostle Paul think of elites and bourgeoisies? He clearly would see them as only useful for supporting the poor so that there could thereby be an equality, as the apostle Paul believed in equality.

The Great White Bluff ... Why Everyone Loses!

Ultimately, in the apostle Paul's understanding of reconciliation he sought all the more for his people's final deliverance, saying, "For I would not, brethren, that ye should be ignorant of this mystery, lest ye should be wise in your own conceits; that blindness in part is happened to Israel, until the fulness of the Gentiles be come in. And so all Israel shall be saved: as it is written, There shall come out of Sion the Deliverer, and shall turn away ungodliness from Jacob: For this is my covenant unto them, when I shall take away their sins" (Romans 11: 25-27), as the apostle Paul wrote to his followers in Rome. On this particular position Fanon and Paul were in partial agreement, for Fanon argued, "The leader, who has behind him a lifetime of political action and devoted patriotism, constitutes [only] a screen between the people and the rapacious bourgeoisie since he stands surely for the ventures of this caste and closes his eyes to their insolence, their mediocrity and their fundamental immorality." To be sure, there is nothing wrong with revolutionary leaders being honoured for their service in guiding and propagating the revolution, especially considering the devotion and peril they take on as frontispieces.

True indeed, however, to Fanon the revolutionary leadership will always be in a precarious situation with regard to the lengths to be taken to achieve revolutionary liberation. All their "hypnotic discursives," all their "Carthagean retreats," all their "Anansian bargains," and "ecstatic eye-wash;" from that point on will ultimately be for the lulling of the masses. Here Fanon took great care to explain the situation, "At the level of individuals, violence is a cleansing force. It frees the native from his inferiority complex and from his despair and inaction; it makes him fearless and restores his self-respect. Even if the armed struggle has been symbolic and the nation is demobilized through a rapid movement of decolonization, the people have the time to see that the liberation has been the business of each and all and that the leader has no special merit" (Fanon 1969: 74).

Malcolm X was even more vehement saying this concerning the Black leadership, "This tokenism … was a program that was designed to protect the benefits of only a handful of handpicked Negroes. And these handpicked Negroes were given big positions, and then they were used to open up their mouths to tell the world, 'Look at how much progress we're making.' He should say, look at how much progress he is making. For while these handpicked Negroes were eating high on the hog, rubbing elbows with white folk, sitting in Washington, D.C., the masses of Black people in this country continued to live in the slum and in the ghetto." He even made very clear concerning these masses in the Black community, "The worst housing conditions in America always exist in the so-called Negro community. Yet the white liberals, who own these run-down houses, force us to pay the highest rent. Faced with this high overhead, we are forced to take in roomers in order to help make up our rent. Our apartments are filled with both relatives and strangers. Our communities soon become overcrowded."

Malcolm X continued that an interesting metamorphosis occurs as a result of this situation, "The overcrowded homes of our community force us to live under some of the worst sanitary conditions imaginable. It becomes almost impossible to practice the rules of good hygiene. And therefore tuberculosis, syphilis, gonorrhoea, and other destructive social diseases are on the rampage throughout our community." "And because there seems to be no hope or no other escape, we turn to wine, we turn to whiskey, and we turn to reefers, marijuana, and even to the dreaded needle – heroin, morphine, cocaine, opium – seeking an escape." Then again, "Unemployment and poverty [also force] many of our people into a life of crime. But the real criminal is in the City Hall downtown, in the State House, and in the White House in Washington, D.C. The real criminal is the white liberal, the political hypocrite."

Malcolm X further explained how White people use these realities experienced in the Black community to further oppress us, saying, "When[ever] they want to suppress and oppress the Black community, what do they do? They take the statistics, and through the press, they feed them to the public. They make it appear that the role of crime in the Black community is higher than it is anywhere else." But, "It's [all] imagery. They use their ability to create images, and then they use these images that they've created to mislead the people. To confuse the people and make the people … actually think that the criminal is the victim and the victim is the criminal." In this situation, as Malcolm X said further, "instead of the sociologists analyzing [things as they actually are] they cover up the real issue, and they use the press to make it appear that [our] people are thieves, hoodlums. No! They are the victims of organized thievery, organized landlords who are nothing but thieves, merchants who are nothing but thieves, [and] politicians who [are] in cahoots with [these] landlords and merchants."

Yet, while he was still in the Nation of Islam, Malcolm X understood, or at least had a plan for, what to do about this particular situation, stating, "The Honorable Elijah Muhammad has the only permanent solution. Twenty million ex-slaves must be permanently separated from our former slavemaster and placed on some land that we can call our own. Then we can create our own jobs. Control our own economy. Solve our own problems instead of waiting on the American white man to solve our problems for us." Still, in delineating this separatist vision he was careful not to thereby endorse segregation, as he explained to his critics, "We reject *segregation* even more militantly than you say you do! We want *separation*, which is not the same! … To *segregate* means to control. Segregation is that which is forced upon inferiors by superiors. But *separation* is that which is done voluntarily, by two equals – for the good of both! The Honorable Elijah Muhammad teaches us that as long as our people here in America are dependent upon the white man, we will always be begging him for jobs, food, clothing and housing. And he will always control our lives, regulate our lives, and have power to segregate us."

Malcolm X was effectively stating here a desire for the Black people of America to have self-determination; a right given to every nationality that has fought for it. For this cause, he championed the idea of Black separatism from the United States in their own struggle for national liberation. "America is a colonial power … She's a twentieth-century colonial power; she's a modern colonial power, and she has colonized [us] African-Americans." "Since [we] were originally Africans, who are now in America not by choice but only by a cruel accident in our history, we strongly believe that African problems are our problems and our problems are African problems." Effectively, "The Honorable Elijah Muhammad teaches us that on our own land we can set up farms, factories, businesses. We can establish our own government and become an independent nation. And once we become separated from the jurisdiction of this white nation, we can then enter into trade and commerce for ourselves with other independent nations."

Nevertheless, Fanon also recognised a problem that arises with the independence of the nation: the bourgeois class begins to assume responsibility for the state, and in many cases is incapable, or at least inexperienced, and therefore re-establishes the conditions of the former colonial power. Here Fanon stated, "The national middle class which takes over power at the end of the colonial regime is an under-developed middle class. It has practically no economic power, and in any case it is in no way commensurate with the bourgeoisie of the mother country … [Effectively, in its] wilful narcissism, the national middle class is easily convinced that it can advantageously replace the middle class of the mother country." That is not to say our Black bourgeoisies are completely incapable, but that the class position without the cultural and economic capital to back it up, only leads inevitably to failure.

That said, a curious puzzle arises when deeply considering the apostle Paul's understanding of the class structure of the early revolutionary movement, we find that he himself identified a class hierarchy for the messianic communities to adhere to: "And God hath set some in the church, first apostles, secondarily prophets, thirdly teachers, after that miracles, then gifts of healings, helps, governments, diversities of tongues." If the apostle Paul acknowledged several different social classes within his own revolutionary vision for social change then who is to say that Allah himself does not identify, or even encourage, the existence of different social classes for different societies? Again, if there was a hierarchy in the early messianic movement then why should there not be hierarchies in society, and even Black society too?

The prosperity preachers will also cry in unison that the current capitalist system is only natural, in that classes have existed in the messianic movement from its inception and have existed in society since the origin of civilisation. Although these ideas will be challenged throughout this series, the understanding that the apostle Paul, being himself a moderately poor man, would not condone competition or permit his followers to be inequitable, shows that at least the idea of social justice was a part of the apostle Paul's revolutionary vision for social change.

Nevertheless, we are still confronted with this discrepancy; the influence of which could produce, and is already producing; various levels of mental, social, and racial complexes as a result. Fanon himself would even articulate how, "The doctrine of cultural hierarchy is thus but one aspect of a systemized hierarchization implacably pursued." Moreover, the cultural narrative, performative, and reproductive of these kinds of systems of unintended dissociation, effectively allow for a social kinetics of superiority and inferiority, thereby showing that those faithful to the apostle Paul's hierarchical structuring would still not undermine his, as important, vision for a socially and economically equal commonwealth.

Consequently, in his letter to the messianic communities of Rome the apostle Paul still chose to complicate the matter further, saying: "For as we have many members in one body, and all members have not the same office: So we, being many, are one body in Christ, and every one members one of another. Having then gifts differing according to the grace that is given to us, whether prophecy, let us prophesy according to the proportion of faith; Or ministry, let us wait on our ministering: or he that teacheth, on teaching; Or he that exhorteth, on exhortation: he that giveth, let him do it with simplicity; he that ruleth, with diligence; he that sheweth mercy, with cheerfulness" (Romans 12: 4-8). These two letters promoting structural hierarchy in the early messianic movement feel shrill, strident, and piercing. They echo throughout the many ages of Christian religious ordination and imperious domination.

However, as I have tried to point out, this was actually a system of unintended dissociation that the apostle Paul did not design disingenuously. In fact, this was not an endorsement of social classes at all, but an ordering and organising of the then disorganised messianic movement. Notwithstanding, while these hierarchical orderings could very well be considered classes, such in fact discounts their revolutionary potential. From a more anarchic perspective such could, by all rights, be considered something far more interesting. Herein, we can see the revolutionary potential of their social superstructure.

An anarchic hierarchy could be constructed either on a federalist structure or a syndicalist structure. A federalist hierarchical structure would be similar to a tribal or governmental structure. The federal bodies would thereby operate to promote and enforce the laws/rules of the social or global body. However, far more potential can be gleaned from the syndicalist hierarchical structure. This is to have in place workplace workers' meetings and neighbourhood consumers' meetings that interact, on one level; and that also hierarchically rise to district level (either village, town, city, or borough); and to regional level (either northwest, southwest, southeast, or northeast); then to national level (including 5 members from each region); then, finally, to international level. This syndicalist chain should essentially go up from the bottom, and not from the top down.

This, in our time, would be the best means of hierarchical structure we could possibly hope for. However, it does beg the question: should such a superstructure be organised on bureaucratic, meritocratic, or technocratic lines? Obviously, in our current "liberalised" institutions we see examples of all three. Yet, in truth, we see examples of none. Monopoly, oligarchy, nepotism, racism, orientalism, sexism, heterosexism, cis-sexism, and various other forms of discrimination pollute society today. In this case, though believing the technocratic option to be the best for us godbodies; I also recognise how hard it will be to implement. Technocracy, similar to meritocracy, is based on the concept of the most qualified rise within the hierarchy; yet, in a technocratic system it is a little more refined. The most technically qualified for a specific position should be the one to get that position. It should be thus regardless of age, class, race, gender, sexual orientation, or any other societal distinction. This is similar to Jim Collins' estimation to not only have the right people on the bus (meritocracy) but the right people in the right seats (technocracy).

However, if we consider again the structure of the later messianic movement we see that it was based primarily on the distortion and corruption of words used by the apostle Paul, nevertheless his actual intended hope was always to produce a system of interdependent offices and vocations within the messianic movement that would function similar to how the human body functions. Just as within the complete functioning of our own bodily composition there are many tasks and many operations, some invisible, some visible, some honourable, some embarrassing, some now co-ordinating with this group, some now co-ordinating with another; yet our entire bodily composition still works in conjunction with the whole to the benefit of all members.

Even so, the apostle Paul's actual vision for the messianic movement (and by extension for Black society as a whole), was that each member would work together for the benefit of all. Though some are skilled at production, others at leading, others at service, and some at manual work, some can operate various devices, some can sell anything, some can entertain, others have mastered a particular art, while still others can retain vast amounts of information and scientific knowledge. All these gifts and abilities were given by Allah to specific individuals. And just as the apostle Paul also said, "If the ear shall say, Because I am not the eye, I am not of the body; is it therefore not of the body? If the whole body were an eye, where were the hearing? If the whole were hearing, where were the smelling?" Even so we should not dismiss the apostle Paul's hierarchical structuring of the early messianic movement, as, in truth, it could not have been avoided. To continue the analogy: we actually do have body parts that are considered more valuable or more honourable than others. It is only when we lose these less valuable members, whether through mutilation or dysfunction, that we appreciate how valuable they really were.

We can see here, through this analogy of the body, certain aspects of the apostle Paul's sociological views about life and nature; that though the analogy actually dates back to Plato, the apostle Paul had an interdependence view of the functionings of society long before Durkheim made it popular. This view and understanding of the interconnection of one part of the body to all the others, and of their relation to how well the body functions as a whole, would effectively allow for those within the messianic movement to adopt traditions of solidarity and brotherhood that transcended *ethnos*, class, gender, and sexuality, and even transcended the ages. It is this holistic view of interconnection that would also lay the ground work for future social and biological theorists throughout Western history. Effectively, within the apostle Paul's revolutionary vision for social change our relation to each other is no longer based on *ethnos*, though *ethnos*, class, gender, and sexuality would ultimately still exist; but on mutual interaction and support. Thus the apostle Paul was trying, in essence, to build among his followers strong familial chords of relation. These chords of relation would effectively allow them to escape the excesses of ethnic, class, gender, and sexual politics to become one family in the Messiah.

The economic aspect of the apostle Paul's revolutionary vision for social change within the early messianic movement was clearly that goods, services, and information be distributed among the brothers and sisters based not on charge but on need. That if a follower within a messianic community had a need they would be able to make known their need to another follower, whether brother or sister, based on what was needed. Thus like an eye needing the help of a hand to see better, it could communicate this information to the hand, who in turn would provide the service. This service, for the sake of equality, would then be provided free of charge as the server would soon, or some other time, require a service from they whom they have just served, thereby maintaining equality.

This vision can further be seen in the following statement, which he made to the messianic communities of Rome, saying, "Be of the same mind one toward another. Mind not high things, but condescend to men of low estate. Be not wise in your own conceits. Recompense to no man evil for evil. Provide things honest in the sight of all men. If it be possible, as much as lieth in you, live peaceably with all men" (Romans 12: 16-18). Herein, Malcolm X asked the very pertinent question concerning the Black community, "What divided us? Our lack of pride. Our lack of racial identity. Our lack of racial pride. Our lack of cultural roots." Yet, he went on to explain why this was so: "Until 1959 [our] image of the African continent was created by the enemies of Africa. Africa was a land dominated by outside powers. A land dominated by Europeans. And as these Europeans dominated the continent of Africa, it was they who created the image of Africa that was projected abroad. And they projected Africa and the people of Africa in a negative image, a hateful image. They made us think that Africa was a land of jungles, a land of animals, a land of cannibals and savages."

Malcolm X further continued, "From [around 1960 onward] the flames of nationalism, independence on the African continent, became so bright and so furious, they were able to burn and sting anything that got in its path." The racial tensions this provoked were strong and Malcolm X understood that. According to Malcolm X this revolutionary spirit sparked by the African nationalists changed the Black people in the West's perception of Africa and thereby it changed their perception of themselves. In this situation, "the three major allies, the United States, Britain, and France, have a problem today that is a common problem. … And that common problem is the new mood that is reflected in the overall division of the Black people within continental France, within the same sphere of England, and also here in the United States. So that – and this mood has been changing to the same degree that the mood on the African continent has been changing. So when you find the African revolution taking place, and by African revolution I mean the emergence of African nations into independence … [it] has absolutely affected the mood of the Black people in the Western Hemisphere."

Malcolm X thereby noted, "You and I are living at a time when there's a revolution going on. A worldwide revolution. It goes beyond Mississippi. It goes beyond Alabama. It goes beyond Harlem. There's a worldwide revolution going on." He also noted that this revolution was a nationalist revolution, stating, "The spirit of nationalism on the African continent [has meant that] the powers, the colonial power, they couldn't stay there. The British got in trouble in Kenya, Nigeria, Tanganyika, Zanzibar, and other areas of the continent. The French got in trouble in the entire French Equatorial North Africa, including Algeria. … The Congo wouldn't any longer permit the Belgians to stay there." At the same time, "when the Black revolution begins to roll on the African continent it effects the Black man in the United States [too] and affects the relationship between the Black man and the white man in the United States."

Deuces are Wild (With No Jokers)

Despite all that has been said so far an argument could still be made that even if we were to accept the idea that the apostle Paul actually was an anti-imperialist revolutionary, there is still hard evidence that he also was yet an apologist for the colonial regime, evidence that itself can be found in his letter to the messianic communities of Rome, where he said to the fellowship, "Wherefore ye must needs be subject, not only for wrath, but also for conscience sake. For for this cause pay you tribute also: for they are God's ministers, attending continually upon this very thing. Render therefore to all their dues: tribute to whom tribute is due; custom to whom customs; fear to whom fear; honour to whom honour. Owe no man any thing, but to love one another: for he that loveth another hath fulfilled the law" (Romans 13: 5-8).

Nonetheless, we also find here a general theme articulated by all the Falashim prophets: all of them crying out for justice in human dealings and interchange, and against the iniquities and inequities of unsociable behaviours and individuals. These prophets would say things like, "Woe to them that devise iniquity, and work evil upon their beds! when the morning is light, they practise it, because it is in the power of their hand. And they covet fields, and take them by violence; and houses, and take them away: so they oppress a man and his house, even a man and his heritage." "Woe to him that increaseth that which is not his! how long? and to him that ladeth himself with thick clay! Shall they not rise up suddenly that shall bite thee, and awake that shall vex thee, and thou shalt be for booties unto them?" "Woe to him that coveteth an evil covetousness to his house, that he may set his nest on high, that he may be delivered from the power of evil! Thou hast consulted shame to thy house by cutting off many people, and hast sinned against thy soul."

So how then do we confront the apostle Paul's assertion "Wherefore ye must needs be subject," and "they are God's ministers"? Let us not forget that the apostle Paul, an international riot-maker and rabble rouser in his own right, most definitely had spies and agents of the state watching him, and imperial police officers reading and examining his letters (as they did with all the apostles and early messianic writers). Remember also, the apostle Paul was a leader in a global revolutionary movement, therefore, any statements of governmental or imperial appeasement should be read as merely Anansian negotiation and strategic dissimulation. Yes, the apostle Paul taught and encouraged honesty and "speaking the truth in love," but imperial methods, historical records, historical context, and implied subtext, all tell a very different story. Therein the social relations and social kinetics of imperialism can be seen: political and cultural suffocation rendered all levels of challenge impotent.

It is for this cause that what we read from the apostle Paul was so easily used by the Roman Imperial officers of the time to say that movements such as the messianic had a duty to give due respect to the existing imperial state, even as it was later used by Roman Catholic clergy to say the same thing these millennia later. Allah was the one who ordained its power, so they say, so it is only ours to give them their due of submission and obedience. The condemnation for such nonsensical guidance was levelled against the imperial power structure of the twentieth century by Malcolm X in his own fiery anti-imperialist retorts: "the American racists know that they can rule … the African American, only as long as we have a negative image of ourselves". And again, "The white man so guilty of white supremacy can't hide his guilt by trying to accuse The Honorable Elijah Muhammad of teaching black supremacy and hate! All Mr Muhammad is doing is trying to uplift the black man's mentality and the black man's social and economic condition in this country."

Accordingly, in spite of the apostle Paul's apparent deference to imperialism, in this very letter to his followers in Rome, there was still discernible certain invisible slippages, certain subterranean confessions, occultly lurking beneath the surface, and attempting their ascent. It is in fact these occult risings that reveal, or dare I say, expose, the apostle Paul's true intentions when he wrote to the Roman believers, "he that loveth another hath fulfilled the law. …Love worketh no ill to his neighbour: therefore love is the fulfilling of the law" (Romans 13: 8, 10). What anarchic statements! In fact, they could even be considered the very basis of anarchism.

Moreover, this was not the first time he made such statements of antinomian (lawless) motivation. The apostle Paul wrote to the messianic communities of Galatia, saying: "For, brethren, ye have been called unto liberty; only use not liberty for an occasion to the flesh, but by love serve one another. For all the law is fulfilled in one word, even this; Thou shalt love thy neighbour as thyself" (Galatians 5: 13, 14). Herein remember, this fulfilling of *all the law* through loving our neighbour was written before the American Revolution and the idea of separating Church from State. Therefore, as stated before, the apostle Paul was not simply talking about all the laws of Moses; he meant *all* legal judgments and requirements.

Having himself an undeniable grasp of the words spoken by the Messiah, when he was confronted by the Herodians (Judean sympathisers with the Roman government) as to whether it was fitting for a Judean to pay taxes to Caesar, he answered, "Shew me the tribute money. And they brought unto him a penny. And he saith unto them, whose is this image and superscription? They say unto him, Cæsar's. Then said he unto them, Render therefore unto Cæsar the things which are Cæsar's; and unto God the things that are God's" (Matthew 22: 19-21). In this, neither the Messiah nor the apostle Paul were advocating the giving of tribute to Caesar or that such was to be instituted as a new Judean tradition from then on, forevermore. What they were really saying was, so long as that empire existed, so long as that power structure existed, they should pay their tribute. If the empire ever fell, however, there would no longer be any need to pay them further tribute (and on an even deeper level: though now Caesar's law exists, follow the law of love and if Caesar's law ever gets abolished we never followed it anyway).

The apostle Paul, therefore, saw the commonwealth of Israel being fulfilled politically in an anarchic system where people would be free to walk in love. So while he may have never instigated an actual revolution (though himself being undeniably a revolutionary), he definitely did not believe in Caesar, or his laws, or his state. He also continued this theme further on in his message to the messianic communities of Rome, saying, "So then every one of us shall give account of himself to God. Let us not therefore judge one another any more: but judge this rather, that no man put a stumblingblock or an occasion to fall in his brother's way. I know, and am persuaded by the Lord Jesus, that there is nothing unclean of itself: but to him that esteemeth any thing to be unclean, to him it is unclean" (Romans 14: 12-14). Thereby, saying, that the structural mechanisms of culture formation that essentially determined the practices, customs, and traditions of the culture, were neither static nor predetermined, but were even then flexible, contestable, and meaningful.

On the other hand, if we look at an institution like Black erotica, which is based substantially on concepts like Black love, free love, and plural love; while it may be a free expression of Black sexuality that has pneumatological potential, it is still heavily judged and stigmatised within society at large. Nevertheless, the main purpose of Black eroticism should centrally be to generate libidinal love, thus producing for the Black community a sensual resurrection. Ultimately, if the Bible intended for the first resurrection to be a mental resurrection, then it would have said that the *noia* or the *noema* was to be resurrected. Instead, it said the psyche was to be resurrected.

For those who do not know, however, the Greek word psyche, back in the classical era, actual meant something more along the lines of: the instinctual drives that produce our external behaviours/activities. In Freudian theory these drives are acknowledged as predominantly sensual drives inspired by the pleasure principle. Herein, we see why in the King James Bible they chose to translate the Greek word *psychikos* as the English word sensual, even if nowadays the word psychic has taken on a far more abstracted meaning. Based on the Freudian interpretation of a sensual, indeed, sexual psyche we can see how the first resurrection was always far more likely to have been considered to be a sensual resurrection.

Accordingly, the godbody prohibition of marriage helps us to fulfil this *eschaton*, or last days' thing, by allowing us to practice a form of free love, or even plural love, in our communities. The truth is, we godbodies need to address this issue of Black eroticism in our philosophy as to not do so would make us hypocrites, using all this language of caring for children and educating the masses in our public discourse while, at the same time, practicing in secret sexual liberality. We either need to add sexual liberality to our public discourse, that is, add the discourse of Black eroticism, or abandon what Allah was trying to teach us and where he was trying to lead us. It should be clear to anyone who gives any serious thought as to why the Father taught us not to marry according to the government that his goal was to promote among us free love practices, thereby sexually liberating us. The fullest expression of this sexual liberation thereby leading us to become sexual objects to the rest of the Black community.

Through this the God would become the sexual object of Black women and the Goddess would become the sexual object of Black men – and though I recognise that the word object has acquired certain negative connotations since Martin Buber (1927) that relate it to the "dehumanising" of human beings, I use it here in the Freudian sense of the word – making us like love objects that can be conduits of their transferences. As the godbody male and godbody female thus become the sexual objects of others they will thereby cause them to discharge sexual energy in the sexual act. Again, if we do not address this issue of sexuality and sexual liberation, we risk our word not being bond, claiming to only be about the family, while, at the same time, loving sex and behaving sexually without admitting that truth. At least if we publicly adopt a discourse of Black eroticism our word becomes bond to truth. Our word also stays *our* bond which others will be able to see in all our ways and actions toward our love objects.

That said, again, the sexual act must always be consensual between both: neither the male nor the female godbody should ever rape anybody, nor allow anybody to rape them. The godbody must therefore practice the use of seduction in their hypererotic behaviour to break down all resisting or reactionary behaviour. In this, there ultimate aim should be to generate within the sexual subject the most powerful force in the universe: sexual energy. That sexual energy will then either be discharged in the sexual act or sublimated into progressive acts – obviously it could also get inhibited once generated if the godbody does not guide them to a fruitful outcome. Therefore, the act of seduction must not be taken lightly. Though the key to Black eroticism must remain seduction it can be both positive and progressive (as it can instigate the liberation of a Black person's sexuality from inhibition or prohibition).

To further clarify, when I use the word seduction it is not here spoken of in the Freudian sense of the word but in the commonsense of the word. Freudian seduction shall henceforth be referred to as perverse seduction in that it takes for granted the idea that an adult, older sibling, or trusted authority will molest a child. Seduction as I use it is still Freudian to a degree, in that it produces within the sexual subject a wish, but it is not *the* Freudian theory of seduction as it has nothing to do with sexual molestation or betrayal. In this version of seduction, the sexual object becomes the sexual fantasy and thereby becomes fetishised – in the sense that they take on mystical attributes. The God becomes sex God to the Black woman thereby allowing her to recognise that the standards of society are, and have always been, artificial and illusory.

It is the central intent of this form of Black eroticism to liberate and empower Black minds, therefore the methodology the God should use to achieve this objective should remain seduction. Still, if one excuses the oversimplification, women will always be better seducers than men. Indeed, any woman can seduce any man she wants, simply by anchoring the constant and consistent exhibition of her body or sexuality to a positive experience he has had. These exhibitions will be like sharp goads on the man's heart, especially when he tries to resist them. Eventually, the pain will become so unbearable that he will be completely in her power. Therefore, a woman should never take anything a man says too seriously as she can easily break him by creating constant and consistent sexual associations and connections, in his mind, to a former positive experience. Obviously, a woman should not have to exhibit the private areas of her body or her sexuality just to seduce a man, however, if she does, it is the most potent form of eroticism she could perform.

True, feminist Jill Johnson did articulate back in the 1980s that, "Feminism at heart is a massive complaint, Lesbianism is the solution … Until all women are lesbians there will be no true political revolution" (Johnson 1985; quoted in Kolawole 1997: 15); yet this was not as hopeless a call to action as it at first may seem. In my own experience, women tend to prefer things like masturbation and lesbianism to male sexual relationships. Herein homosexuality may not be as genetic in the case of women as it is in the case of men. The truth is, women are generally better at sexual expression than men, knowing in many cases instinctively how to sexually please both men and women. Add to that the emotional support, friendship, bonding, and compassion they are able to receive from other women, and the overall shittiness of men when they show or demonstrate the slightest bit of sexual independence or freedom and it makes it that much easier for women to leave the game entirely, either practicing lesbianism, or identifying as bisexual or pansexual. In certain cases, obviously, those women will continue to date or have relationships with men, however, in a lot of cases that will only be due to the stigma of self- or same-sex pleasure, or due to the wealth and power of men in the current world system.

Essentially, while what Johnson was hoping for may at first have seemed somewhat impossible, especially considering how far a cry it is from the "you don't choose to be gay" rhetoric, choosing instead the promotion of using love for political ends. Still, building on from her, a far more powerful war cry would be for *all* women to practice the lifestyle of free love and thus free themselves from the burden of marriage and the various other standards imposed on them by church and state. On the other hand, if we were to look deeper into the conception of Black eroticism, which is based fundamentally on Black love, free love, and plural love, it is definitely more than what marriage could ever be: it is a free expression of hypereroticism that possesses a high pneumatological potential.

We should also remember that according to Freud eroticism is the most powerful force in the universe. For this reason, I have been fighting so hard to allow Black women to express their own eroticism or hypereroticism. Imagine if you will that all Black men were suddenly to possess a superpower: the ability to transmit their thoughts to other Black men. Imagine that only Black men possessed this superpower and that they could use it to uplift the Black community. Now imagine that society continued to stigmatise and demonise this superpower as evil and ignorant. Imagine they also labelled those who used this superpower as corrupt and backward. Would any of this stop Black men from using their superpower to liberate Black people? Well, *all* women have a genuine superpower with eroticism, yet for some reason they despise their superpower unable to appreciate how great it is.

The truth is, men, even with all our political and social power, are unable to handle a very erotic woman, especially as women can stir up in us all the spiritual, social, cultural, martial, political, economic, scientific, and athletic genius we require in life through sublimation. As to the notion that *all men really despise and will never respect* these types of women: Napoleon Hill, one of the great heroes of this current alpha-male revival, had this to say in his most seminal, "One of America's most able businessmen frankly admitted that his attractive secretary was responsible for most of the plans he created. He confessed that her presence lifted him to heights of creative imagination, such as he could experience under no other stimulus" (Hill 2004: 217). Still, those determined to continue the argument may say that this was the man's secretary, with no placement at all in the so-called whorearchy; but sexual objectification is sexual objectification regardless of what position you hold in society.

Herein those at the lower levels of society, and of the whorearchical pyramid, may face great stigmatisation from those at the higher levels of both, but the men these higher level women assume despise them in many cases not only do not fall into these women's dehumanising stereotype of men, but actually *secretly adore* these women. As a man myself, a man who has done time in prison surrounded by a multitude of other men, I can attest: one of the most essential things that got us through our time in prison was not our wives or girlfriends as such. Although, obviously, they were extremely important, in every single case, they were also the cause of our biggest pain and difficulty, even when they gave us what we would call "naked flicks."

What really got us inmates through our time in prison, again, in every cis-hetero case, was what we called "pussy books", the softcore porno magazines featuring pictures of fully naked women. On the so-called whorearchy pyramid those types of women would represent the top (Cam Girls), but I guarantee this, during our time in prison – though I am obviously unable to speak for all of us – the vast majority of us cis-hetero males saw these same types of women as sacred, yes sacred, for their willingness to pose in those types of pictures. Why? Because without them prison would have been a more literal hell. We may change our tune when we get out and are among our N!gg@s, true indeed, but that is a different story altogether.

Again, these types of women, to us, had and have always had, a superpower. Yet rather than encouraging these types of women, and particularly those within the Black community, to use their superpower for their own liberation we join with White society, most likely jealous of the Black woman's predominance in this particular field; and condemn them whenever they do use it. Now some women may think that eroticism is not that great a superpower, but I disagree. It is an amazing, wonderful, and incredible superpower. The only real reason I can think of as to why so many women currently look down on such a force is because they have not yet learned to reject society's stigmatisation of it and use it to empower themselves.

Yet for any seductionist, *whether male or female*, the one overriding aim they desire is to give the greatest amount of erotic pleasure to those they are interacting with. Moreover, their seduction will always be deviant, though it should ultimately be a beneficial deviance, used to liberate and not to oppress. Their seduction must also be unoffendable, therefore it will not be discouraged by bad results but strengthened by them. Seduction by name means there is resistance. Indeed, with no resistance it is not seduction but arousal. They should not feel too discouraged because of these resistances though, as in their desire to produce in that person, male or female, the greatest amount of sexual pleasure they could possibly have, they will have effectively revealed to them the very face of Allah, which is al-Muhibb (the Libidinal One).

All these ideas take on a deeper meaning in the writings of the apostle Paul, who having his own transgressive doctrine, sought to re-educate the various ethnicities of the empire, saying, "Wherefore remember, that ye being in time past Gentiles in the flesh, who are called Uncircumcision by that which is called the Circumcision in the flesh made by hands; That at that time ye were without Christ, being aliens from the commonwealth of Israel, and strangers from the covenants of promise, having no hope, and without God in the world: But now in Christ Jesus ye who sometimes were far off are made nigh by the blood of Christ. For he is our peace, who hath made both one, and hath broken down the middle wall of partition between us" (Ephesians 2: 11-14). The kind of indoctrination the apostle Paul was here trying to impart to the messianic communities of Ephesus was with the sole aim of allowing them to see that they belonged to a separate kingdom or commonwealth from that of Imperial Rome: the very commonwealth of Israel itself.

What is quite telling in these statements is a hidden absence, one that is quite marked, though is rarely considered. The original message of both the Baptist and the Messiah was the message of the kingdom of God, yet the concept itself is noticeably and painfully rare outside of the gospels. More common are the ideas of: kingdom of Christ, kingdom of the Son, heavenly kingdom, etc. While it may be implied that they are all the same thing, it is clear that Paul's perception of the kingdom was of the imminent earthly rule of the Son of David over the commonwealth of Israel. Again, the apostle Paul was not hoping and fighting for a heavenly rule for the Messiah: in his view, as in that of the early messianic movement, the Messiah already ruled in a heavenly kingdom. What the apostle Paul was hoping and fighting to do was spread the Messiah's earthly kingdom among the various nations of the world.

Ultimately, such an interpretation, combined with all we have considered so far, opens up to us the deeper levels of the apostle Paul's ideological agenda. Firstly, the apostle Paul believed wholeheartedly in ethnic, gender, sexual, economic, and class equality. Secondly, his hope and desire for class equality did not necessarily mean to him the end of hierarchy altogether, just a redefinition of the social kinetics of hierarchy. To the apostle Paul hierarchy should be official (that is, based primarily on the office/positon the person occupied) and not personal (that is, based primarily on the calling, destiny, or charisma of the individual), so to him authority rested in the seat not the personality. Thirdly, the apostle Paul believed the function of society, and particularly of the messianic communities in society, was to operate like the human body, each part playing the role best suited to it similar to what we in our day would call a division of labour.

Here, we can understand that an honestly Pauline ideology would have to acknowledge a societal division of labour, however, one that is substantially different from our own in that it would not have its basis in the market forces of supply and demand, forces which ultimately commodify human beings (and everything else in existence); thereby placing our value and worth as human beings at the mercy of said forces. Herein also we see that the key ideological issues of the world today: hierarchisation, legitimisation, racialisation, sexualisation, heterosexualisation, cis-sexualisation, pornification, gendering, the division of labour, uneven social and industrial development, and the damaging of environmental integrity; are in fact not the real problem. The world can maintain all these divisions and the social kinetics they each entail and still be a just, fair, and perfect society. The problem is, and has been since modernity: commodification – that is, determining intrinsic value by market value. Though in feudal times value was determined by so-called divine right (another fallacy) in our time value, and thereby power, is determined only by market forces, which the apostle Paul would never have agreed to.

Even Malcolm X shared Paul's authentic views for most of his public career, while feeling, at the same time, that they could also be problematised, especially when it came to the issue of Black and White race-relations in America, saying, "Why, when all of my ancestors are snake-bitten, and I'm snake-bitten, and I warn my children to avoid snakes, what does that *snake* sound like accusing *me* of hate-teaching?" The apostle Paul in considering the Black and White races of the empire of Rome, felt that there was an opportunity to unify due to the Messiah's sacrifice, "For he is our peace, who hath made of both one, and hath broken down the middle wall of partition between us; Having abolished in his flesh the enmity, even the law of commandments contained in ordinances; for to make in himself of twain one new man, so making peace."

Ultimately, in walking this path of the anti-imperialist we must learn to supersede all legal articulation, and all the discourses used as their justification, so as to allow for their cultural valorisation. The apostle Paul said, "Not that we are sufficient of ourselves to think any thing as of ourselves; but our sufficiency is of God; Who also hath made us able ministers of the new testament; not of the letter, but of the spirit: for the letter killeth, but spirit giveth life" and such an outlook is the definition of revolutionary. Incidentally, Lenin made a point about most revolutionary movements that could be quite pertinent here: he said that their opportunist section have a tendency, at the height of their public acceptability, to deny the more utopian elements of their initial programme, even "as Christians, after their religion had been given the status of state religion, 'forgot' the 'naiveté' of primitive Christianity with its democratic, revolutionary spirit" (Lenin 2014: 81).

A further example of this revolutionary spirit is detectable in Fanon's heroic efforts, arguing that, "This rediscovery, this absolute valorization almost in defiance of reality, objectively indefensible, assumes an incomparable and subjective importance. On emerging from these passionate espousals, the native will have decided, 'with full knowledge of what is involved,' to fight all forms of exploitation and of alienation of man. At this same time, the occupant, on the other hand, multiplies appeals to assimilation, then to integration, to community" (Fanon 1964: 43). Fanon was here presenting a methodology for decolonising mind, body, and spaces, and for valorising the traditional narratives, performatives, and reproductives.

Yet even here the apostle Paul can help us, for inasmuch as he served and followed Allah, he was also willing to acknowledge "the working of his mighty power, Which he wrought in Christ, when he raised him from the dead, and set him at his own right hand in the heavenly places, Far above all principality, and power, and might, and dominion, and every name that is named, not only in this world, but also in that which is to come" (Ephesians 1: 19-21). What a valorisation! Yet remember, these were not simply spiritual (that is astral) principalities, powers, might, and dominions, these were earthly, corporeal, and imperial rulers. Moreover, each of these imperial rulers governed over their own small or large territory within the Roman Empire.

This idea is brought into even sharper focus by the words the apostle Paul said to the messianic communities in the city of Rome: "Now I say that Jesus Christ was a minister of the circumcision for the truth of God, to confirm the promises made unto the fathers: And that the Gentiles might glorify God for his mercy; as it is written, For this cause I will confess to thee among the Gentiles, and sing unto thy name. And again he saith, Rejoice, ye Gentiles, with his people. And again, Praise the Lord, all ye Gentiles; and laud him, all ye people. And again, Esaias saith, There shall be a root of Jesse, and he that shall rise to reign over the Gentiles; in him shall the Gentiles trust" (Romans 15: 8-12); this one is of particular interest to us here for, to give a more in-depth quotation:

> *"And there shall come forth a rod out of the stem of Jesse, and a Branch shall grow out of his roots: And the spirit of the Lord shall rest upon him ... And righteousness shall be the girdle of his loins, and faithfulness the girdle of his reins. The wolf also shall dwell with the lamb, and the leopard shall lie down with the kid; and the calf and the young lion and the fatling together; and a little child shall lead them. And the cow and the bear shall feed; their young ones shall lie down together: and the lion shall eat straw like the ox. And the sucking child shall play on the hole of the asp, and the weaned child shall put his hand on the cockatrice' den. They shall not hurt nor destroy in all my holy mountain; for the earth shall be full of the knowledge of the Lord, as the waters cover the sea. And in that day there shall be a root of Jesse, which shall stand for an ensign of the people; to it shall the Gentiles seek" (Isaiah 11: 1-10).*

This union of animals and people that anticipates the kingdom of God upon the earth is, in essence, a learning of empathic interconnection and communal support and interdependence. These figurative realities, however, are not that far from the truth of nature; for as the apostle James also said, "every kind of beasts, and of birds, and of serpents, and of things in the sea, is tamed, and hath been tamed of mankind" (James 3: 7). Pyotr Kropotkin also reminds us, "Association is found in the animal world at all degrees of evolution; … But, in proportion as we ascend the scale of evolution, we see association growing more and more conscious. It loses its purely physical character, it ceases to be simply instinctive, it becomes reasoned. With the higher vertebrates it is periodical, or is resorted to for the satisfaction of a given want – propagation of the species, migration, hunting, or mutual defence."

Moreover, a relation to such "liberation fauna" could potentially allow us to become a lot more zoopathic in our interchanges with nature. For example, as Kropotkin noted, in a "migration of fallow-deer which I witnessed on the Amur, and during which scores of thousands of these intelligent animals came together from an immense territory, flying before the coming deep snow, in order to cross passed before my eyes, I saw Mutual Aid and Mutual Support carried on to an extent which made me suspect in it a feature of the greatest importance for the maintenance of life, the preservation of each species, and its further evolution." This statement gives further credence to Mimi Sheller's understanding of how even nature "can take on quite widely differing symbolic meanings, can support highly varied social performances, and can become the material grounds for opposed 'productions of space' (Lefebvre 1991: 90)." It is therefore our empathy with nature, its flora and fauna, that gives us true connection.

Even nineteenth century social theorist and Marxist thinker Fredrick Engels confessed in his debates with the revisionist

Eugen Dühring concerning the Darwinian discussion that "the idea of the struggle for existence … Darwin himself admitted, has to be sought in a generalization of the views of the economist and theoretician of population, [Thomas] Malthus, and that the idea therefore suffers from all the defects inherent in the priestly Malthusian ideas of over-population." But "the *fact* [that this struggle] exists also among plants can be demonstrated to him by every meadow, every cornfield, every wood; and the question at issue is not what it is to be called, whether 'struggle for existence' or 'lack of conditions of life and mechanical effects,' but how this fact influences the preservation or variation of species."

These kinds of "contested natures," ultimately reveal their subaltern identity, not only in the obvious fact of the struggles of cornfields and meadows, but also in the mutual aid and mutual interaction in cornfields and meadows. For it is impossible to look at these beautiful expressions of plant life and not see their sociable togetherness and unity, while their invisible struggles and fights for survival and maintenance, though real, are virtually insignificant to the senses. Indeed, Sheller took this concept even further, stating how "wild forests[,] as ciphers of subaltern historicity … have an erotic force that transcends the scale of human lives and disrupts the ordering projects of states. Plants are protean, imperialistic, bent on reproduction by exercising a kind of agency from below that is both generative and destructive" (Sheller 2012: 193).

Moreover, as Engels further stated in a letter to his friend P. L. Lavron, "The whole Darwinist teaching of the struggle for existence is simply a transference from society to living nature of Hobbes's doctrine of *bellum omnium contra omnes* [war of all against all] and of the bourgeois-economic doctrine of competition together with Malthus's theory of population." Claiming, that even, "In recent times the idea of natural selection was extended … and the variation of species conceived as a result of the mutual interaction of adaptation and heredity, in which process adaptation is taken as the factor which produces variations, and heredity as the preserving factor." Effectively, to him the Darwinian contribution was best summed in what he accomplished for science, "Darwin brought back from his scientific travels the view that plant and animal species are not constant but subject to variation." And this in itself was a remarkable achievement for his time. However, "It is true that in doing this Darwin attributed to his discovery too wide a field of action, made it the sole agent in the alteration of species and neglected the causes of the repeated individual variations, concentrating rather on the form in which these variations become general; but this is a mistake which he shares with most other people who make any real advance."

True indeed, "Animals [may] change the environment by their activities in the same way, even if not to the same extent, as man does, and these changes [may] in turn react upon and change those who made them. In nature nothing takes place in isolation. Everything affects and is affected by every other thing," so that, "Even the mere contemplation of previous history as a series of class struggles suffices to make clear the utter shallowness of the conception of this history as a feeble variety of the 'struggle for existence.'" For which cause, "In my opinion, the social instinct was one of the most essential levers of the evolution of man from the ape." (And though most Black people may not currently accept the idea that humanity evolved from apes, the fossil record itself is quite undeniable. The fossils of the earliest hominidae – humanlike beings – bear huge similarities to large primates, while the later ones come closer and closer to Homo sapiens people as we know them).

Kropotkin also agreed with Engels, showing how, "Association and mutual aid are the rule with mammals. We find social habits even among the carnivores, and we can only name the cat tribe (lions, tigers, leopards, etc.) as a division the members of which decidedly prefer isolation to society, and are but seldom met with even in small groups. And yet, even among lions 'this is a very common practice to hunt in company.' The two tribes of the civets (*Viverridæ*) and the weasels (*Mustelidæ*) might also be characterized by their isolated life, but it is a fact that during the last century [that is, the nineteenth century] the common weasel was more sociable than it is now". And, "apart from a few exceptions, those birds and mammals which are not gregarious now, were living in societies before man multiplied on the earth and waged a permanent war against them, or destroyed the sources from which they formerly derived food."

Furthermore, Kropotkin also had this to say concerning wildlife, "numberless are those which live in societies, either for mutual defence, or for hunting and storing up food, or for rearing their offspring, or simply for enjoying life in common … though a good deal of warfare goes on between different classes of animals, or different species, or even different tribes of the same species, peace and mutual support are the rule within the tribe or the species; and that those species which best know how to combine and to avoid competition, have the best chances of survival and of a further progressive development." These kinds of environments of recognition, these matrices of communication, will be essential for us Black people in our great pursuit of late modern unification.

He further stated on the subject, "When I explored the Vitim regions in the company of so accomplished a zoologist as my friend Polyakoff […] We both were under the fresh impression of the *Origin of Species*, but we vainly looked for the keen competition between animals of the same species which the reading of Darwin's work had prepared us to expect … We saw plenty of adaptations for struggling, very often in common, against the adverse circumstances of climate, or against various enemies, … but even in the Amur and Usuri regions, where animal life swarms in abundance, facts of real competition and struggle between higher animals of the same species came very seldom under my notice, though I eagerly searched for them."

To finalise the subject he then stated "mutual aid is as much a law of animal life as mutual struggle, but that, as a factor of evolution, it most probably has a far greater importance, inasmuch as it favors the development of such habits and characters as insure the maintenance and further development of the species," for "even in those few spots where animal life teemed in abundance, I failed to find – although I was eagerly looking for it – that bitter struggle for the means of existence, *among animals belonging to the same species*, which was considered by most Darwinists (though not always by Darwin himself) as the dominant characteristic of struggle for life, and the main factor of evolution."

As to the apostle Paul's doctrine of ethnicities, that is completely different from his doctrine concerning wealth. While he did tolerate the ethnic diversity of Imperial Rome he did not seem to tolerate wealth obsession. Though, at that time, far less oppressive than chattel slavery would prove to be in later years, ethnicity was not as important to the apostle Paul's anti-imperialism as the contradictions of wealth, for which cause he said in the same letter to the evangelist Timothy, "Charge them that are rich in this world, that they be not highminded, nor trust in uncertain riches, but in the living God, who giveth us richly all things to enjoy; That they do good, that they be rich in good works, ready to distribute, willing to communicate".

The apostle Paul was essentially saying here that in the Roman Empire those with wealth should share their wealth with a spirit of simplicity and humility. Also feeling the *ethnos* should learn to see each other as brothers and sisters in messianism. Malcolm X, on the other hand, did not believe ethnic brotherhood/sisterhood was really possible in the American Empire. To him this was not due to White racism as such, but due mostly to Black accommodation, trying desperately to please and suck-up to White people, "The *ignorance* we of the black race here in America have, and the *self-hatred* we have, they are fine examples of what the white slavemaster has seen fit to teach to us. Do we show the plain common sense, like every other people on this planet Earth, to *unite* among ourselves? No! We are humbling ourselves, sitting-in, and begging-in, trying to unite with the slavemaster!"

Again, that is not to say that Malcolm X had nothing but animosity towards White people, just that he knew from painful experience what they were capable of, "The North's liberals have been for so long pointing accusing fingers at the South and getting away with it that they have fits when they are exposed as the world's worst hypocrites." Indeed, with the "white Southerner, you can say one thing – he is honest. ... The advantage of this is the Southern black man never has been under any illusions about the opposition he is dealing with." Therefore, Malcolm X's general message was simple: "let us, the black people, *separate* ourselves from this white man slavemaster, who despises us so much! You are out here begging him for some so-called *'integration'*! But what is this slavemaster white, *rapist*, going about saying! He is saying *he* won't integrate because black blood will *mongrelize* his race!" Herein Malcolm X developed an anti-imperialism not of integration, like with Dr. King and the apostle Paul, but was much more of a separatist in seeking what he believed to be a true independence for Black Americans.

That said, to bring a close to this chapter, and to consolidate everything we have learned about the apostle Paul throughout so far, I wish to share with you what I believe to have effectively been, for all intents and purposes, the apostle Paul's Luthenian message of sacrifice; a message he shared with the messianic communities of Corinth for the purpose of inspiration. Hopefully it will give you strength just like it has given me all these years:

"I speak as concerning reproach, as though we had been weak. Howbeit whereinsoever any is bold, (I speak foolishly,) I am bold also. Are they Hebrews? so am I. Are they Israelites? so am I. Are they the seed of Abraham? so am I. Are they ministers of Christ? (I speak as a fool) I am more; in labours more abundant, in stripes above measure, in prisons more frequent, in deaths oft. Of the Jews five times received I forty stripes save one. Thrice was I beaten with rods, once was I stoned, thrice I suffered shipwreck; a night and a day I have been in the deep; In journeyings often, in perils of waters, in perils of robbers, in perils by mine own countrymen, in perils by the heathen, in perils in the city, in perils in the wilderness, in perils in the sea, in perils among false brethren; In weariness and painfulness, in watchings often, in hunger and thirst, in fastings often, in cold and nakedness. Beside those things that are without, that which cometh upon me daily, the care of all the churches. Who is weak, and I am not weak? who is offended, and I burn not?" (2Corinthians 11: 21-29).

As someone who has been a revolutionary for many years now I can say from a revolutionary perspective: this is what real revolution looks like.

Know When to Fold'em

Seeing now the true interrelation between the doctrine of the apostle Paul and the teachings we share within the godbody movement, it may be necessary, at this point, to state that though we godbodies are by personal definition practitioners of Islam, we are more so, in actual fact, a supra-religious culture, not dogmatically holding to the beliefs or ideas of any religion, or to the god of any religion. We choose instead to reserve any force of commitment to our own outlook, philosophy, beliefs, and practices.

For this cause, I feel that in most, if not all, points the godbody movement has been denied its constitutional rights under US — and most Western — laws, to freedom of peaceful assembly. Being ourselves practitioners of peaceful assembly, we do not feel, and have not felt, it necessary to tie ourselves down to any particular religion, but to attend whichever religious grouping we feel most connects with our spiritual and personal views. Here we are also most vehement, for we are unwilling to sacrifice our own right to freedom of assembly within our cipher. Our own religious connection is not based on formal institutions, but on how we practice our lessons culturally.

At the same time, the major thing that separates us godbodies from most of the mainstream of Black movements is not our radical views on race, sex, violence, deviance, or spirituality; but as Malcolm X said, that we "believe in one God, and [we] believe that that God had one religion, has one religion, always will have one religion. And that that God taught all of the prophets the same religion, so there is no argument about who was greater or who was better; Moses, Jesus, Muhammad, or some of the others. All of them were prophets who came from one God. They had one doctrine, and that doctrine was designed to give clarification of humanity" (Malcolm X 1989: 157). Godbodyism thereby embraces a supra-religious outlook and worldview; while also acknowledging that that which has been passing in our time as prophetic is, in actual fact, merely just utterance as given by Allah's grace, or delusion as given by personal vanity.

The current Christian prejudice against the Prophet Ali Muhammad is based primarily on ignorance, having its basis in the Crusades and not on any genuine antithesis in theoretics. Islam is actually, in essence, a messianic sect, and had it have come after the Reformation, it would have been seen as no different from the Adventists or the Jehovah's Witnesses. As to the three fundamental difficulties within Islamic Christology: that of his incarnation, death, and resurrection; these issues, though troublesome, are no reason at all for the tremendous abuse given to the Muslim world to try to choke them out of existence.

As to the central stone of contention, that of Muhammad's prophethood; in the early years of the messianic movement, it is well known and understood that several prophets and apostles arose among the faithful. These pre-Nicaean prophetic movements were unfortunately too dangerous to continue after Nicaea and so were altogether snuffed out by the religious establishment of the time. Those who chose to maintain this authentic legacy were thus forced to retreat into the wilderness of Egypt, the last vestige of spiritual expression, to join one of the monasteries there. Then, finally, at the fall of Rome, messianic spirituality and prophecy were eradicated completely from the culture, as was anything in any ways contrary to the orthodox Catholic views, as gnostic or potentially heretical and therefore illegal.

With prophecy thus outlawed and forbidden in both Western and Eastern Churches, and with the messianic movement by that time having decayed into an endless parade of useless doctrinal councils and nonsensical imperial tyre-kicking; Allah had no choice but to look outside of the Church to find one who he could speak to and work through. It is within this setting that we find the man Ali Muhammad. According to Malcioln, he was "an Arab of the Kuraish tribe of western Arabia. His grandmother was Ethiopian. His wife Amiva was also of the Kuraish tribe. His father Abdallah died shortly after the boy was born in 571 A.C.E. Therefore, Ali Muhammad was brought up by his uncle Abu Talib. This was six years after the reign of Justinian. Some scholars place Muhammad's birthplace at Mecca, others give Medina."

During that time, the vast majority of the lands of North and East Africa, and the Near Eastern Orient, were Christian: whether Orthodox, Nestorian, Arian, or Gnostic. Mecca, at that time, was one of the few islands of idolatry left in the world, having idols all housed in the Kabah. Yet if Mecca was one of the few islands of idolatry left in the world it was not due to ignorance. The Bedouin Arabs, who controlled trade along the Silk Road between Europe and the Far East, all had their own tribal deities and tribal superstitions: including the statues, amulets, talismans, and idols they believed in. These Bedouin Arabs, who came to the Kabah to visit their deities, gave to Mecca great wealth and prestige through trade.

At the age of 24, Muhammad married a rich Catholic widow much older than himself, named Khadija. He apparently loved Khadija deeply and took no other wives during her lifetime. For the next 12 years he became a shrewd and wealthy businessman and trader, travelling across the Syrian trade routes with his uncle Abu Talib and the two sons of Abu Talib. Malcioln further argued that Muhammad was described by those who knew him "as a likeable good-natured individual, and rather charismatic. He was also somewhat of a poet, but was not considered to be a learned man, even during those times. [Still,] he did practice writing religious verses in rhyming couplets with enough repetition to allow his semiliterate congregants to readily memorize his poems" (Malcioln 1996: 195).

It was also during his journeys that Muhammad clearly got acquainted with various Gnostic, Arian, and Kabalic traditions (most of them from non-canonical sources). These would have been what inspired him in his late 30s to retreat into the Arabian desert for the purpose of living an ascetic life. By the time he reached his 40s the life of a businessman had lost its charms and Muhammad could see the decadence of the Meccan elite, not to mention the fallen state of the Kabah, which was a shrine originally built by Abraham himself to honour the monistic principle the Muslims now call *al-tawhid*. At that point, Muhammad went into a cave on Mount Hirah to ask this monistic principle to send to his people a prophet like those of the ancient Falashim. It was then, according to legend, that Muhammad received a vision of the archangel Gabriel (Jibril), who told him that he would be that prophet he was praying for, and began to open up to him the Quran, a scroll known and hidden in the mind of Allah long before the creation of the universe began.

When Muhammad first announced to the people of Mecca that he was a prophet sent by Allah to restore them to the traditions and culture of their Abrahamic ancestors, they first began to taunt him, provoke him, slander him, and persecute him; then they stripped all his followers – of which after four years there were only 15 – of their titles and all their property. This response makes sense as his philosophy and message of political and religious monism was a threat to the political and religious elite of Mecca, and the established system that was in operation at that time, a system that allowed Mecca and its elites to become very wealthy. Indeed, Muhammad's only followers in those earlier years were slaves and women, for whom he was a champion. Still, after eleven years of prophesying he ended up with very little to show for his efforts but exclusion, poverty, and persecution. The very existence of the movement itself would not have been possible without several communal exiles. The final one, called by the Muslims the hegira (meaning migration, but also connoting exodus), was to Yathrib, a city populated by several Falashic, Arabic, and Sabean tribes.

Yet as Malcioln further explained, "It is written that when Muhammad fled his native Mecca in 622 A.C.E. (the hegira), he was much concerned about one reversal in particular. The Hebrew people from whom Muhammad had learned so much were expected to follow his new version of their old religion." It is for this cause that one of the Prophet's earlier messages while in the city of Yathrib, which he renamed Medina, was, "Say: We believe in Allah and (in) that which has been revealed to us, and (in) that which was revealed to Abraham, and Ishmael and Isaac and Jacob and the tribes, and (in) that which was given to Moses and Jesus, and (in) that which was given to the prophets from their Lord, we do not make any distinction between any of them and to Him do we submit" (Quran 2: 136). Indeed, the Prophet believed all prophecy represented a continuum, a line going all the way back to Abraham himself.

What is also interesting in this verse is the Prophet's reference to the historically silenced voice of Ishmael. The deafeningly loud absence of Ishmael's presence in all biblical accounts of the continuum actually speaks volumes. The Prophet's mention of Ishmael as within the prophetic tradition thereby identified his corporeal presence and valorised his embodied historicity. It also corrected the erasure of his sacramentality thereby giving sanctity to his deviant presence. As the Prophet saw himself as the confirmation and seal of prophecy (itself also a kind of transfigured deviance), he did not wish to exclude any he thought to be true prophets, within the Falashim prototype.

To carry this idea a little further the apostle John said in the epistle of Revelations that "the testimony of Jesus is the spirit of prophecy" (Revelation 19: 10); a basic idea that obviously had its roots in an incident that occurred when the Messiah was at his house teaching, "And John answered him, saying, Master, we saw one casting out devils in thy name, and he followeth not us: and we forbad him, because he followeth not us. But Jesus said, Forbid him not: for there is no man which shall do a miracle in my name, that can lightly speak evil of me. For he that is not against us is on our part. For whosoever shall give you a cup of water to drink in my name, because ye belong to Christ, verily I say unto you, he shall not lose his reward" (Mark 9: 38-41). A far cry from the words of former President Bush.

The question therefore becomes, what was the Prophet's view of Jesus? The Prophet said, "We gave Jesus, son of Mary, clear arguments and strengthened him with the Holy Spirit. Is it then that whenever there came to you a messenger with what your souls desired not, you were arrogant? And some you gave the lie to and others you would slay" (Quran 2: 87). Again, as the apostle John also said in his first general epistle, "I have not written unto you because ye know not the truth, but because ye know it, and that no lie is of the truth. Who is a liar but he that denieth that Jesus is the Christ? He is antichrist, that denieth the Father and the Son", to which the Quran answered, "When the angels said: O Mary, surely Allah gives thee good news with a word from Him (of one) whose name is the Messiah, Jesus, son of Mary, worthy of regard in this world and the Hereafter, and of those who are drawn nigh (to Allah)." Again, "The Messiah disdains not to be a servant of Allah, nor do the angels who are near to Him. And whoever disdains His service and is proud. He will gather them all together to Himself" (Quran 3: 45, 46; 4: 172).

Thus, in all this, we see the hand of Allah; for the apostle Paul also explained, "Wherefore I give you to understand, that no man speaking by the Spirit of God calleth Jesus accursed: and that no man can say that Jesus is the Lord, but by the Holy Ghost. Now there are diversities of gift, but the same Spirit. And there are differences of administrations, but the same Lord. And there are diversities of operations, but it is the same God which worketh all in all. But the manifestation of the Spirit is given to every man to profit withal. For to one is given by the Spirit the word of wisdom; to another the word of knowledge by the same Spirit; To another faith by the same Spirit; to another the gifts of healing by the same Spirit; To another the working of miracles; [and] to another prophecy;" all by the same Spirit and based on the same standard. Again, when he said, "no man can say that Jesus is the Lord, but by the Holy Ghost", he was showing that prophecy, one of the gifts of the Holy Ghost, is identifiable through acknowledging the Messiah's dominion.

Conversely, according to various sources, the Falashim of Medina, would challenge the Prophet Muhammad concerning his birth-right, saying, "You were born of Ishmael, but we are descendants of Isaac, Jacob, and Judah, who received the blessings of Abraham." To which the Prophet apparently answered, "Do not blessings (rather) follow the righteous, as they will dwell in Jannah enjoying that which their Lord has bestowed on them? For every child is born in innocence. It is his parents who turn him Judaic, messianic, or atheistic." Further, the Prophet also apparently spoke these words to them, saying, "O People of the Book, indeed Our Messenger has come to you, making clear to you much of that which you concealed of the Book and passing over much. Indeed, there has come to you from Allah, a Light and a clear Book, Whereby Allah guides such as follow His pleasure into the ways of peace, and brings them out of darkness into light by His will, and guides them to the right path" (Quran 5: 15, 16). However, according to Malcioln, "They scorned 'the confused utterances of the Arab prophet in all that pertained to Judaism.'"

Essentially, "The Prophet allowed the Bene Israel to go unmolested for some time. He kept hoping that they would not have to be forced to join him. Muhammad, may Allah be gracious unto him, wished that the Hebrews would eventually become a segment of the Islamic community, but the years passed and the possibility faded. The Hebrews refused to give accreditation to the new religion. With no Hebrews among the Moslem chiefs of staff, and none in the Islamic hierarchy, with just a few in the lower echelons of the fighting forces, Muhammad said, 'We shall spread Islam with fire, and the sword.' Bekr, his disciple and commander-in-chief of the fighting forces, [also] suggested that Islam discard its Hebraic liturgical penchants" (Malcioln 1996: 197). From this point on the Prophet broke away from the Falashism, changed the qibla (focus and direction of prayer) from Jerusalem to the Kabah, changed the murad al-salat (expected number of prayers) from three to five, changed the yaum al-sawm (time of fasting) from the Yom Kippor to the month of Ramadan, and changed the hajj (focus of travel) from Jerusalem to Mecca. Around about that time he began to unify all the Christian and non-Christian Arabian tribes into one body.

It is then that Allah revealed to the Prophet, "You are the best nation raised up for men: you enjoin good and forbid evil and you believe in Allah. And if the People of the Book had believed, it would have been better for them. Some of them are believers but most of them are transgressors." Therefore, do not be afraid to "fight in the way of Allah against those who fight against you but be not aggressive. Surely Allah loves not the aggressors. And kill them wherever you find them, and drive them out from where they drove you out, [for] persecution is worse than slaughter. And fight not with them at the Sacred Mosque until they fight with you in it; so if they fight you (in it), slay them. Such is the recompense of the disbelievers. But if they desist, then surely Allah is Forgiving, Merciful. And fight them until there is no persecution, and religion is only for Allah. But if they desist, then there should be no hostility except against the oppressors" (Quran 3: 110; 2: 190-193).

True, this message may be a little too deviant for our oversensitive, "turn the other cheek" ears, yet we are still willing to let the police and the military use violence and slaughter for the preservation of this oppressive White supremacist system and for the cause of this White supremacist system. What the Prophet was basically saying was that instead we should be willing to fight and die to defend our own monistic system. Indeed, "Muhammad's strongest attraction in Islam, it is said, is the perfect brotherhood and equality before God of all his believers, regardless of color, origin, or status. Being himself dark-skinned, Ali Muhammad tried to protect the dark-skinned members of the faith." Even so, it has been incumbent upon all Muslims, from the time of the Prophet to this day, to fight against all forms of oppression and division, whatever form they actually come in.

Effectively, through these verses the Prophet was able to create a thearchic army willing to fight as a unified body, possessing a strong sense of destiny, and with the fear of nothing but Allah in their hearts. This martially embodied unit represents today a form of transfigured deviance, having a deep history of fighting against oppression that goes back for centuries. At the same time, let me bring back again the key determinant factor, "fight in the way of Allah against those who fight against you but be not aggressive." Those who fight against you but be not aggressive! The truth is, they are actually a lot further from the aggressive, religion by the edge of a sword, image most Westerners have of them.

Nevertheless, the apostle Paul still said concerning true messianism: "the righteousness which is of faith speaketh on this wise, Say not in thine heart, Who shall ascend into heaven? (that is, to bring Christ down from above:) Or, Who shall descend into the deep? (that is, to bring up Christ again from the dead.) But what saith it? The word is nigh thee, even in thy mouth, and in thy heart: that is, the word of faith, which we preach; That if thou shalt confess with thy mouth the Lord Jesus, and shalt believe in thine heart that God hath raised him from the dead, thou shalt be saved." To which the Prophet Muhammad said,

"The People of the Book ask thee to bring down to them a Book from heaven; indeed they demanded of Moses a greater thing than that, for they said: Show us Allah manifestly. So destructive punishment overtook them on account of their wrongdoing. Then they took the calf (for a god), after clear signs had come to them, but We pardoned this. And We gave Moses clear authority. And We raised the mountain above them at their covenant. And We said to them: Enter the door making obeisance. And We said to them: Violate not the Sabbath; and We took from them a firm covenant. Then for their breaking their covenant and their disbelief in the messages of Allah and their killing the prophets wrongfully and their saying, Our hearts are covered; nay, Allah has sealed them owing to their disbelief, so they believe not but a little. And for their disbelief and for their uttering against Mary a grievous calumny. And for their saying: We have killed the Messiah, Jesus, son of Mary, the messenger of Allah, and they killed him not, nor did they cause his death on the cross, but he was made to appear to them as such. And certainly those who differ therein are in doubt about it. They have no knowledge about it, but only follow a conjecture, and they killed him not for certain: Nay, Allah exalted him in His presence. And Allah is ever Mighty, Wise. And there is none of the People of the Book but will believe in this before his death; and on the day of Resurrection he will be a witness against them."

These Quranic verses have troubled many Jews and Christians historically (obviously for different reasons); however, in the Maulana Muhammad Ali translation of the Quran is provided the beginnings of a reconciliation, at least with Christianity. According to Ali, "The words *ma salabu-hu* do not negative Jesus' being nailed to the cross; they negative his having expired on the cross as a result of being nailed to it." While this may be true and helpful, perhaps even more helpful in explaining the deeper meaning behind these verses is The Coptic Apocalypse of Peter, where it speaks of the apostle Peter's receiving an astral vision of the actual crucifixion of Jesus, yet at the same time, above the cross was a disembodied Jesus absolutely thrilled and laughing at the event.

Here is how the events were recounted by the apostle Peter,

> *"When he had said those things, I saw him apparently being seized by them. And I said, 'What am I seeing, O Lord? Is it you yourself whom they take? And are you holding on to me? Who is this one above the cross, who is glad and laughing? And is it another person whose feet and hands they are hammering?'*

> *The Savior said to me, 'He whom you see above the cross, glad and laughing, is the living Jesus. But he into whose hands and feet they are driving the nails is his physical part, which is the substitute. They are putting to shame that which is in his likeness. But look at him and me.'*

> *But I, when I had looked, said, 'Lord, no one is looking at you. Let us flee this place.' But he said to me, 'I have told you, "Leave the blind alone!" And notice how they do not know what they are saying. For the son of their glory, instead of my servant, they have put to shame.'" (Ehrman 2005: 80).*

What we can clearly see therefore is that the Prophet being most likely trained and guided in a gnostic tradition, as is also clear in several other gnostic references throughout the Quran that he could never have gotten without having been trained directly from the gnostic tradition (the books and writings themselves having been for the most part lost or buried). Moreover, it is only through and due to the discovery of the Nag Hammadi Library that we can see this gnostic influence in the Prophet's own development. It is for these reasons that I seriously doubt that this man, who clearly admired martyrdom and giving your life for Allah, could have had in mind anything less than the common Christian interpretation with his verses. And if he believed that Allah still exalted the Messiah after his death then he thereby also believed in the Messiah's resurrection.

Finally, the Prophet had this to say concerning Mary his mother, "She said: How can I have a son and no mortal has yet touched me, nor have I been unchaste? He said: So (it will be). Thy Lord says: It is easy to Me; and that We may make him a sign to men and a mercy from Us. And it is a matter decreed" (Quran 19: 20, 21). As to the question of the Messiah's incarnation the Prophet had this to say, "The likeness of Jesus with Allah is truly as the likeness of Adam. He created him from dust, then said to him, Be, and he was" (Quran 3: 59). Even so, concerning his ministry he also said, "I have come to you with a sign from your Lord, that I determine for you out of dust the form of a bird, then I breathe into it and it becomes a bird with Allah's permission, and I heal the blind and the leprous, and bring the dead to life with Allah's permission; and I inform you of what you should eat and what you should store in your houses. Surely there is a sign in this for you, if you are believers" (Quran 3: 49).

What we can gather from this brief history is that after the first 11 years of Muhammad's prophethood, he and his followers became nothing more than exiles and political refugees; however, after the second 11 years of Muhammad's prophethood he had effectively become the de facto ruler of Arabia, keeper and cleanser of the Kabah, and the founder of a movement that in time would stretch from India and Albania in the East, all the way to Senegal and Iberia in the West, and everywhere in between. "After the Prophet's death, Abu Bekr, also known as Bakr, became the first Caliph (632-634). His short reign dealt with homogenizing tribes who had never been accustomed to a central authority controlling them from a power base far away. ... Bekr died in 634 A.C.E. Omar succeeded him and reigned until he was stopped in 644. He wrested Egypt and Syria from the Byzantine, Persia, and Iraq. He [essentially] died one year before his armies reached the borders of India and China."

In all, we can here see, not only the genuine prophethood of Muhammad, but also our right to claim Muhammad as one of our own prophets. In fact, the only reason why Muhammad was rejected from the body of Catholic prophets and saints was due to the historical foundations of Catholicism itself. Here the doctrine of Irenaeus of Lyon was adopted into the body of saintly doctrines. Still, Irenaeus incorporated the ideas of a centralised hierarchy, ideological supremacy, Christian patriotism, and intellectual authoritarianism into Catholic Christianity; while Muhammad incorporated the ideas of an informal structure, ideological assimilation, ultra-monotheism, and intellectual development into his vision for Orthodox Islam.

Conclusion

In concluding this beginning of interpretations into what the godbody movement understands to be the truest, if not at least purest and most consistent, perspective of what the early messianic movement presented in their communities, and how the apostle Paul tried to build through them a social and ecclesiastical platform; I now hereby state that this Black thearchist movement is in effect a truer representation of that original messianic vision and reality that existed in its early days. It has been the misinterpreting of this vision by generations of unknowledgeable people that has essentially brought on the current doom of modernity.

If, however, any non-Five Percenter was troubled by any of the ideas and lessons I dropped throughout this book I must say that they were all the development of decades of thorough research and many years of connection to the street life. While I currently may be more connected to academia than the streets, my years of apprenticeship in the streets and in prison made me quite aware of the realities of what we are. I never lost that mentality. My hope therefore is to show you, particularly the intellectuals among you, the reality and value of our theology, ideology, and culture. That we are far more than simply criminals and thugs. We do have a philosophical basis that is not only respectable but also credible. In essence, this book is for you, in the hopes that you will see our vision and join us in elevating our communities to a place of genuine divinity.

Series Postscript

Though this series is and will be very controversial throughout, especially for one who is a self-proclaimed Black theologian. Nevertheless, considering that the Black thearchy I have herein sought to promote to the world is neither a corrupt authoritarian, nor a chaotic utopian, system, but in fact an already existing ghetto movement, our motive is not the ultimate overthrow of existing bourgeois society. All we seek is merely the defending of our actually existing culture, traditions, and doctrinal viewpoints, even as they currently stand, and not the allowing of any modernist standards or opinions to corrupt them or contaminate any of our existing doctrinal interpretations; regardless of the level of persecution we receive for carrying them.

In modern society the main and central differentiation between revolutionary deviance and criminal malevolence is a matter of internal perspective: just like "one man's terrorist is another man's freedom fighter." Distinction is also perceptible through a person's level of internal consciousness. Or to better clarify, the central disparity between a criminal and a freedom fighter *is* their level of consciousness. Yet using such a reductionist simplification one could draw the further conclusion that all that really distinguishes a freedom fighter from the divine is, in this case, their level of *habba* (libido). Here, through altering perspectives we can hopefully attain to a raising of *habba*, and thereby of divinity in the street life.

Ultimately, through strengthening the social forces of ghetto culture we can effectively begin the process of abolishing White privilege, and overthrowing this whole corrupt system of White supremacy. Herein, the godbody movement provides a wealth of guidance, and access to many lessons that may prove quite complex. For this cause, if you currently wish to learn more about our movement (I get paid nothing for this endorsement), feel free to write to the address below:

> The Allah School in Mecca
> 2122 7th Avenue
> New York, NY 10027
> USA

Also be sure to let them know that it was a book in this series that inspired you to join. Once they have been informed as to your true intentions they should be willing to give you everything you need to be an enlightened part of this movement.

Lastly, I have really enjoyed writing this book; and as a part of my *Black Divinity Series* it has been a key facet and aspect of my life's work as a theologian and biblical scholar. For this cause, I currently make this final request: that if you have gained or learned anything you feel to be of value please remember to leave a review on the platform from which you purchased this book. Small things like that help authors like me gain wider readership and validation for our efforts. They also give us the opportunity to hear some of stories of those we have touched with our work. Thank you for your support, much love and peace.

Attention African American Theologians!!!

What if Everything you Thought you Knew About the End Times Was Wrong?

Eschatological Judgments is the second instalment in Shahidi Islam's *Black Divinity Series*. With the world manipulating Black history we need to find a way to get to our truth. To learn more click the Buy button to get it now.

Eschatological Judgments
Buy Now

Bibliography

Abraham, N (1994); "Notes on the Phantom a Complement to Freud's Metapsychology." In N. T. Rand (Ed), *The Shell and the Kernel*; University of Chicago Press.

Abraham, N (1994); "The Phantom of Hamlet or The Sixth Act preceded by The Intermission of 'Truth'." In N. T. Rand (Ed), *The Shell and the Kernel*; University of Chicago Press.

Abraham, N & Torok, M (1994); "Mourning or Melancholia: Introjection Versus Incorporation." In N. T. Rand (Ed), *The Shell and the Kernel*; University of Chicago Press.

Abron, J. M (2005); "'Serving the People': The Survival Programs of The Black Panther Party." In C. E. Jones (Ed), *The Black Panther Party [Reconsidered]*; Black Classic Press.

Adogame, A (2011); "Introduction." In A. Adogame (Ed), *Who is Afraid of the Holy Ghost: Pentecostalism and Globalization in Africa and Beyond*; Africa World Press.

Afrika, L (2013); Dr Llaila Afrika We Are Different; http://m.youtube.com/watch?v=r6aaP6Ynoj4, accessed in May 2014.

Albert, M (2004); *Parecon: Life After Capitalism*; Verso

Alexander, M (2011); *The New Jim Crow: Mass Incarceration in the Age of Colorblindness*; The New Press.

Aptheker, H (1996); "Maroons Within the Present Limits of the United States." In R. Price (Ed), *Maroon Societies: Rebel*

Slave Communities in the Americas; The John Hopkins University Press.

Asante, M. K (2003); "The Afrocentric Idea." In A. Mazama (Ed), *The Afrocentric Paradigm*; Africa World Press, Inc.

Asante, M. K (2013); "Afrocentricity Imagination and Action." In V. Lal (Ed), *Afrocentricity Imagination and Action*; Multiversity & Citizens International.

Ashby, M (2003); *Sacred Sexuality: Ancient Egyptian Tantric Yoga The Neterian Guide to Love, Sexuality, Marriage, Relationships and the Secrets of Sexual Energy Cultivation, Sublimation, and Spiritual Enlightenment*; Sema Institute of Yoga.

Avineri, S (1968); *The Social & Political Thoughts of Karl Marx*; Cambridge University Press.

Baudrillard, J (2012); *Simulacra and Simulation*; The University Press.

Bauman, Z (2016); *Liquid Modernity*; Polity Press.

Bauman, Z (2003); *Identity Conversations with Benedetto Vecchi*; Polity Press.

Ben-Jochannan, Y (2002); *The Need for a Black Bible*; Black Classic Press.

Bey, M (2020); *Anarcho-Blackness: Notes Toward a Black Anarchism*; AK Press.

Blackburn, R (1988); *The Overthrow of Colonial Slavery 1776-1848*; Verso Books.

Brandchaft, B, Doctors, S, and Sorter, D (2010); *Toward an Emancipatory Psychoanalysis: Brandchaft's Intersubjective Vision*; Routledge.

Brown, F, Driver, S and Briggs, C (2014); *The Brown-Driver-Briggs Hebrew and English Lexicon*; Hendrickson Publishers.

Buber, M (2008); *I and Thou*; Simon & Schuster.

Callinicos, A (2003); *An Anti-Capitalist Manifesto*; Blackwells Publishing Ltd.

Chittick, W (1989); *The Sufi Path of Knowledge*; State University of New York Press.

Chiu, C-Y, Leung, A. K-Y. & Hong, Y-Y (2011); "Cultural Processes: An Overview." In A. K-Y. Leung, C-Y Chiu & Y-Y Hong (Eds), *Cultural Processes A Social Psychological Perspective*; Cambridge University Press.

Churton, T (2015); *Gnostic Mysteries of Sex: Sophia the Wild One and Erotic Christianity*; Inner Traditions.

Collins, J (2006); *Good to Great and the Social Sectors: A Monograph to Accompany Good to Great*; Random House Business.

Collins, J (2020); *Good to Great*; [ONLINE] Available at: https://www.audible.co.uk/webplayer?asin=147359202X&contentDeliveryType=SinglePartBook&ref_=a_minerva_cloudplayer_147359202X&overrideLph=false&initialCPLaunch=true. [Accessed 07/12/2023].

Collins, J & Porras, J. I (2005); *Built to Last: Successful Habits of Visionary Companies*; Random House Business Books.

Cone, J. H (2012); "Theology's great sin: silence in the face of white supremacy." In *The Cambridge Companion to Black Theology*, eds. Dwight N. Hopkins and Edward P. Antonio; Cambridge University Press.

Cone, J. H (2018); *Black Theology and Black Power: Fiftieth Anniversary Edition*; Orbis Books.

Cone, J. H (2020); *A Black Theology of Liberation: 50th Anniversary Edition*; Orbis Books.

Davis, D (1984); *Slavery and Human Progress*; Oxford University Press.

Degnbol-Martinussen, J, Engberg-Pedersen, P (2005) *Aid: Understanding International Development Cooperation*. London: Zed Book Ltd.

Diop, A (1991); *Civilization or Barbarism*; Lawrence Hill Books.

Douglas, K. B (1999); *Sexuality and the Black Church: A Womanist Perspective*; Orbis Books.

Durkheim, E (2014) *The Rules of Sociological Method: And Selected Texts on Sociology and its Method*. New York: Free Press.

Durkheim, E, Mauss, M (2009); *Primitive Classification*; Taylor & Francis.

Ehrman, B. D (2003); *Lost Scriptures: Books that Did Not Make It into the New Testament*; Oxford University Press, Inc.

Elias, N (2014) *The Civilizing Process*. Oxford: Blackwell Publishing.

Engberg-Pedersen, P, Gibbon, P, Raikes, P, Udsholt, L (1996) *Limits of Adjustment in Africa: The Effects of Economic Liberalization, 1986-94*. Suffolk: James Curry Ltd., Heinemann, Reed Publishing.

Engels, F (1947); *Anti-Dühring Herr Eugen Dühring's Revolution in Science*; Progress Publishers.

Foner, P (2002); *The Black Panther Speaks*; Da Capo Press.

Fanon, F (1964); *Toward the African Revolution*; Grove Press.

Fanon, F (1965) *A Dying Colonialism*; Grove Press.

Fanon, F (1969); *The Wretched of the Earth*; Penguin Books.

Fanon, F (2008) *Black Skin, White Masks*; Pluto Press.

Feuerstein, G (1998); *Tantra: The Path of Ecstasy*; Shambhala Publications, Inc.

Foucault, M (1998) *The History of Sexuality Vol. 1: The Will to Knowledge*; Penguin Books.

Foxe, J (2001); *Foxe's Book of Martyrs*; Bridge-Logos Publishing.

Franco, J. L (1996); "Maroons and Slave Rebellions in the Spanish Territories." In R. Price (Ed), *Maroon Societies: Rebel Slave Communities in the Americas*; The John Hopkins University Press.

Freeden, M (2013); "The Morphological Analysis of Ideology." In M. Freeden, L. T. Sargent, and M. Stears (Eds),

The Oxford Handbook of Political Ideologies; Oxford University Press.

Gahlin, L (2007); *Egypt: Gods, Myths and Religion*; Anness Publishing Ltd.

Gentles-Peart, K (2016); *Romance with Voluptuousness: Caribbean Women and Thick Bodies in the US*; University of Nebraska Press.

Gilroy, P (1999); *The Black Atlantic: Modernity and Double Consciousness*; Verso.

Gladwell, M (2002); *The Tipping Point: How Little Things Can Make a Big Difference New Edition*; Abacus.

Gladwell, M (2009); *Outliers: the Story of Success*; Penguin Books.

Gleick, J (1998); *Chaos: The Amazing Science of the Unpredictable*; Vintage Books.

Goldman, E (1911); *Marriage and Love*; Mother Earth Publishing Association.

Gordon, L (2012); "Requim on a Life Well Lived: In Memory of Fanon." In N. Gibson (Ed), *Living Fanon: Global Perspectives*; Palgrave Macmillan.

Grady-Willis, W. A (2005); "The Black Panther Party: State Repression and Political Prisoners." In C. E. Jones (Ed), *The Black Panther Party [Reconsidered]*; Black Classic Press.

Gramsci, A (1971); *Antonio Gramsci: Selections from the Prison Notebooks*; Lawrence &Wishart Ltd.

Graves-Brown, C (2010); *Dancing for Hathor: Women in Ancient Egypt*; Continuum Books.

Green, E (2020); *Dark Mind Control Techniques in NLP: Powerful Mindset, Language, Hypnosis, and Frame Control*; Modern Mind Media.

Grinker, R, Lubkemann, S, Steiner, C (2010); *Perspectives on Africa: A Reader in Culture, History, and Representation Second Edition*; Blackwell Publishing Ltd.

Hardt, M, Negri, A (2000) *Empire*; Harvard University Press.

Harman, C (1999); *Economics of the Madhouse*; Bookmarks Publications Ltd.

Harrison, L (2002); "On Cultural Nationalism." In P. Foner (Ed), *The Black Panther Speaks*; Da Capo Press.

Harvey, D (2006); *Limits to Capital*; Verso Book.

Hawass, Z (2006); *The Royal Tombs of Egypt*; Thames & Hudson Ltd.

Hayes, F. W, III, Francis, K. A, III (2005); "'All Power to the People': The Political Thought of Huey P. Newton and The Black Panther Party." In C. E. Jones (Ed), *The Black Panther Party [Reconsidered]*; Black Classic Press.

Herring, G (2006); *Christianity: From the Early Church to the Enlightenment*; Continuum International Publishing Group.

Heywood, A (2017); *Political Ideologies: An Introduction*; Palgrave.

Hill, N (2004); *Think and Grow Rich Revised and Expanded by Dr Arthur R. Pell*; Vermillion London.

Hudson, M (2021) *Super Imperialism: The Economic Strategy of American Empire Third Edition*. Dresden: ISLET-Verlag.

Ibn Katheer Dimashqi, H (2006); *Book of the End: Great Trials and Tribulations*; Maktaba Dar-us-Salam.

Imseis, A (2010); "Speaking Truth to Power: On Edward Said and the Palestinian Freedom Struggle." In A. Iskandar and H. Rustom (Eds), *Edward Said: A Legacy of Emancipation and Representation*; University of California Press.

Intelexual Media (2023); *A Short History of Masturbation*; [ONLINE] Available at:
https://www.youtube.com/watch?v=0aoY6Ihjips.
[Accessed 29/11/2023].

Jackson, S. A (2009); *Islam and the Problem of Black Suffering*; Oxford University Press.

Jacobs, M (1992); *Key Figures in Counselling and Psychotherapy: Sigmund Freud*; Sage Publications Ltd.

Johnson, O. A (2005); "Explaining the Demise of The Black Panther Party: The Role o Internal Factions." In C. E. Jones (Ed), *The Black Panther Party [Reconsidered]*; Black Classic Press.

Jones, W. R (1998); *Is God a White Racist? A Preamble to Black Theology*; Beacon Press.

Josephus, F (2013); *The Works of Josephus: New Updated Edition*; Hendrickson Publishers.

Karenga, M (1989); *Introduction to Black Studies*; University of Sankore Press.

Katz, A (2008); *The Holocaust: Where Was God? An Inquiry into the Biblical Roots of Tragedy*; Burning Bush Press.

Keen, D (2012); *Useful Enemies: When Waging Wars is More Important than Winning Them*; Yale University Press.

King, M. L, Jr (1986); *A Testament of Hope*; HarperCollins Publishers.

King, M. L, Jr (1992); *I Have A Dream; Writings and Speeches That Changed the World*; HarperCollins Publishing.

Koester, C (2014); *Revelation*; Yale University Press.

Koestler, A (1976); *The Thirteenth Tribe*; Random House, Inc.

Kolawole, M. E. M (1997); *Womanism and African Consciousness*; African World Press.

Kropotkin, P (2002); *Anarchism*; Dover Publications Inc.

Kropotkin, P (2006); *Mutual Aid: A Factor of Evolution*; Dover Publications Inc.

Kumar, D (2012); *Islamophobia and the Politics of Empire*; Haymarket Books.

Lady Gaga (2009); *Poker Face (Official Music Video)*. [ONLINE] Available at: https://www.youtube.com/watch?v=bESGLojNYSo. [Accessed 31/12/2023].

Lenin, V (1968); *V. I. Lenin Selected Works*; Lawrence and Wishart Ltd.

Lenin, V (2010); *Imperialism: The Highest Stage of Capitalism*; Penguin Books.

Lenin, V (2014); *State and Revolution*; Haymarket Books. Square Press, Inc.

Lenin, V (2020); *What Is to Be Done? Burning Questions of Our Movement*; Science Marxiste.

lil' bill (2023); *How Black Elites LIE to Us*; [ONLINE] Available at: https://www.youtube.com/watch?v=Uu-X_E8cwaA. [Accessed 29/11/2023].

Littlewood, R (2006); *Pathology and Identity: The Work of Mother Earth in Trinidad*; Cambridge University Press.

Lizokin-Eyzenberg, E & Shir, P (2021); *Hebrew Insights From Revelation*. Israel: Jewish Studies for Christians.

Luxemburg, R (2004); *The Rosa Luxemburg Reader*; The Monthly Review Press.

Lyotard, J (1986); *The Postmodern Condition: A Report on Knowledge*; Manchester University Press.

MacCulloch, D (2010); *A History of Christianity*; Penguin Random House.

Mackenzie-Grieve, A (1968); *The Last Years of the English Slave Trade Liverpool 1750-1807*; Frank Cass & co. Ltd.

Malcioln, J (1996); *The African Origins of Modern Judaism*; Africa World.

Marx, K (1986); *Capital Volume I*; Lawrence &Wishart Ltd.

Marx, K (1958); *Selected Works vol 3*; Foreign Languages Publishing House.

Maxwell, M (1998); *Revelation: Doubleday Bible Commentary*; Bantam Doubleday Dell Publication Group, Inc.

M'Bantu, A, Muller, G (2013); *The Ancient Black Hebrews and Arabs*; Pomegranate Publishing.

McHugo, J (2019); *A Concise History of Sunnis & Shi'is*. London: Saqi Books.

McRobbie, A (2008); *Pornographic Permutations*; Routledge.

Meiu, G. P (2011); "'Mombasa morans': embodiment, sexuality and Samburu men in Kenya." In S. Tamale (Ed), *African Sexualities: A Reader*; Pambazuka Press.

Meyer, M, W (1992); *The Gospel of Thomas: The Hidden Saying of Jesus*; Harper.

Moltmann, J (1993); *Theology of Hope: On the Ground and Implications of a Christian Eschatology*. Minnesota: Fortress Press.

Muhammad, E (1965); *Message to the Blackman of America*; Muhammad's Temple of Islam No. 2.

Newton, H (2002); *The Huey P. Newton Reader*; Seven Stories Press.

Nkrumah, K (2006); *Class Struggle in Africa*; Panaf Books.

Nkrumah, K (2009); *Consciencism Philosophy and Ideology for De-Colonization*; Monthly Review Press.

Nkrumah, K (2022); *Neo-Colonialism: The Last Stage of Imperialism*; African People's Conference.

Nye, J S, Jr (2004); *Soft Power: The Means to Success in World Politics*; Public Affairs Books.

Nzegwu, N (2011); "'Osunality' (or African eroticism)." In S. Tamale (Ed), *African Sexualities: A Reader*; Pambazuka Press.

Patterson, O (1996); "Slavery and Slave Revolts: A Sociohistorical Analysis of the First Maroon War, 1665-1740." In R. Price (Ed), *Maroon Societies: Rebel Slave Communities in the Americas*; The John Hopkins University Press.

Philo (2016); *The Works of Philo: Complete and Unabridged New Updated Edition*; Hendrickson Publishers Marketing, LLC.

Raja, M (2020); *Decolonizing Literary Theory: Some Tentative Thoughts | Zahiriyya and Bataniyya Philosophy*; [ONLINE] Available at: https://www.youtube.com/watch?v=Ez7UZUCM8wo. [Accessed 06/12/2023]

Rand, N. T (1994); "New Perspectives in Metapsychology: Cryptic Mourning and Secret Love." In N. T. Rand (Ed), *The Shell and the Kernel*; University of Chicago Press.

Rand, N. T (1994); "Secrets and Posterity: The Theory of the Transgenerational Phantom." In N. T. Rand (Ed), *The Shell and the Kernel*; University of Chicago Press.

Roberts, A (2011); *Evolution The Human Story*; Dorling Kindersley Limited.

Roberts, J. D (2012); "Dignity and destiny: black reflections on eschatology." In *The Cambridge Companion to Black Theology*, eds. Dwight N. Hopkins and Edward P. Antonio. Cambridge: Cambridge University Press.

Rogers, K (1976); *The Gambler*. [ONLINE] Available at: https://www.youtube.com/watch?v=7hx4gdlfamo. [Accessed 31/12/2023].

Rowland, C (1985); *Christian Origins: An Account of the Setting and Character of the most Important Messianic Sect of Judaism*; SPCK.

Said, E (2003) *Orientalism*. London: Penguin Books.

Saraswati, S (2012); *Kundalini Tantra*; Yoga Publications Trust.

Sardar, Z, Abrams, I (2012); *Introducing Chaos: A Graphic Guide*; Icon Book Ltd.

Schimek, J-G (2011); *Memory, Myth, and Seduction: Unconscious Fantasy and the Interpretive Process*; Routledge.

Seale, B (2002); "The Ten-Point Platform and Program of the Black Panther Party." In P. Foner (Ed), *The Black Panther Speaks*; Da Capo Press.

Seleem, R (2004); *The Egyptian Book of Life*; Watkins Publishing London.

Seligman, C. G (1966); *Races of Africa*; Oxford University Press.

Sheller, M (2012); *Citizenship From Below: Erotic Agency and Caribbean Freedom*; Duke University Press.

Singh, N. P (2005); "The Black Panthers and the 'Undeveloped Country' of the Left." In C. E. Jones (Ed), *The Black Panther Party [Reconsidered]*; Black Classic Press.

Skousen, M (2017); *The Big Three in Economics: Adam Smith, Karl Marx, and John Maynard Keynes*; Routledge.

Smif-N-Wessun (1995); "Home Sweet Home." In *Dah Shinin'* [CD]. New York: Wreck Records, Nervous, Inc.

Smif-N-Wessun (1995); "PNC." In *Dah Shinin'* [CD]. New York: Wreck Records, Nervous, Inc.

Snoop Doggy Dogg (1994); *Doggystyle*; Death Row Records.

St. Augustine (1958); *City of God*; Bantam Doubleday Dell Publishing Group, Inc.

Stourton, E (2005); *In the Footsteps of Saint Paul*; Hodder Headlin Ltd.

Strong, J (1990); *The New Strong's Exhaustive Concordance of the Bible*; Thomas Nelson Publishers.

Strachey, J (1936); *The Theory and Practice of Socialism*; Victor Gúllancz Ltd.

The Holy Bible: King James Version (2002); Michigan: Zondervan.

The Holy Qur'an: Maulana Muhammad Ali Translation (2002); Ohio: Ahmadiyya Anjuman Isha'at Islam Lahore Inc.

Torok, M (1994); "The Illness of Mourning and the Fantasy of the Exquisite Corpse." In N. T. Rand (Ed), *The Shell and the Kernel*; University of Chicago Press.

Turman, E. M (2018); "Heaven and Hell in African American Theology." In *The Oxford Handbook of African American Theology*, eds. Katie G. Cannon and Anthony B. Pinn; Oxford University Press.

Turner, L (2011); "Fanon and the Biopolitics of Torture: Contextualizing Psychological Practices as Tools of War." In N. Gibson (Ed), *Living Fanon: Global Perspectives*; Palgrave Macmillan.

Tyldesley, J (2011); *The Penguin Book of Myths & Legends of Ancient Egypt*; Penguin Books.

Umoja, A. O (2005); "Set Our Warriors Free: The Legacy of The Black Panther Party and Political Prisoners." In C. E. Jones (Ed), *The Black Panther Party [Reconsidered]*; Black Classic Press.

Van Loon, H (1960); *The Story of Mankind*; Washington Square Press, Inc.

Vanee, L (2023); *End the Genocide* [ONLINE] Available at: https://www.facebook.com/reel/1584869658715687. [Accessed 17/12/2023].

Wacquant, L (2016) "Bourdieu, Foucault, and the Penal State in the Neoliberal Era." In D. Zamora & M. C. Behrent (Eds), *Foucault and Neoliberalism*. Cambridge: Polity Press.

Watterson, B (2013); *Women in Ancient Egypt*; Amberley Publishing.

Williams, D. S (1993); *Sisters in the Wilderness: The Challenge of Womanist God-Talk*; Orbis Books.

Williams, D. S (2011); "Black Theology and Womanist Theology." In D. N. Hopkins & E. P. Antonio (Eds), *The Cambridge Companion to Black Theology*; Cambridge University Press.

Williams, J (1928); *Hebrewisms of West Africa From the Nile to the Niger with the Jews*; Africa Tree Press.

X, M (1968); *The Autobiography of Malcolm X*; Penguin Books.

X, M (1989); *Malcolm X: The Last Speeches*; Pathfinder.

X, M (2004); *Why I am Not an American*; Citizens International.